HOW TO FEEL BETTER…
REALISTICALLY

by

Geoff Pridham

WISDOM PUBLISHING

Copyright © 2023 Geoff Pridham

All rights reserved.

Cover illustration by Geoff Pridham

ISBN: 978-0-6459378-1-7

CONTENTS

1. HOW TO ENJOY YOUR LIFE BETTER … 1
2. HOW TO REALISTICALLY IMPROVE YOUR FEELINGS … 11
3. OTHER REALISTIC WAYS TO FEEL BETTER … 35
4. THE SUBCONSCIOUS … 55
5. OTHER PEOPLE … 71
6. LOOKING FOR THE BAD … 87
7. FIXING AND IMPROVING THINGS … 101
8. "UNFIXABLE" WORLD PROBLEMS … 121
9. HUMOR … 137
10. DREAMS, INTERESTS AND WORTHWHILE ACTIVITIES … 145

THE FINAL WORD … 155

1. HOW TO ENJOY YOUR LIFE BETTER

"If you feel happy then you are happy."

Everyone wants to be happy and enjoy their lives better. How can you do that?

There sure are plenty of books and articles out there telling you what to do. The experts are up to your eyeballs! But do you see everyone getting happier in our world today? The opposite seems to be the case.

Let me solve this for you: happiness is a state of mind. It's how you feel. If you can arrange things so that you feel better then you will be happier. How can you do this? Before I answer that, let's look at what doesn't work.

WHAT DOESN'T WORK ☹

1. Trying to Arrange a Perfect Life ✦

Some people put a lot of effort into making their life perfect, but it cannot work. The reason? You might be able to improve your life but it will never be perfect. That is an impossible dream. Something will always be wrong… or go wrong!

What about aiming for something a bit more possible: just trying to improve your life? Would that work? Well, yes and no. It will work in the sense that you can improve some things in your life, and these could make you feel better. But, on the other hand, you won't be able to improve everything, and this means that you will still feel bad about some parts of your life. Also, as many people have found, when you do get some improvements they make you happy only for a while. You soon get used to them and return to your normal way of feeling, which is not so great!

You might choose to get back on the treadmill and work to improve the next thing in your life, so that you can feel better for another short period of time. And then get back on the treadmill again for another short period of better feelings. And so on until you die, or at least get tired of trying! But there are better ways.

2. Getting Things 📱 + 🖥 + 🚗 (Or 👗 + 👠 + 👜)

What about getting things? Can this make you feel better? We all know someone who chases after the next best thing: a smarter phone, a bigger TV, a faster car. (Or the latest fashion dress, glamorous shoes, a new handbag…) It makes them feel better for a while. But the happiness does not last. They are soon chasing after the next big item. It's another treadmill that never ends.

3. Putting Your Happiness in the Hands of a Special Person 💕

What about putting your happiness in the hands of another person? If you can find the right person then can't you live happily ever after with them? It's just a dream. Real people have their real flaws and limitations, which you are certain to notice over time.

How can a flawed human being make you happy forever?

Some people try to push their flawed partner back into shape, hoping that true happiness will return. But this is a hope that can never be fulfilled. No matter how much your partner tries to change to meet your dream requirements their own humanity will continue to exert itself and push back into view. After all, they are a person too, with their own interests and nature. This cannot be hidden forever.

4. Relying on Your Friends 😎😄😃

If you can't find eternal happiness with that special partner then maybe you can spend some quality time with your friends. Can this be made to work?

Not if you want to feel better all of the time. First of all, you cannot spend all your time with your friends doing fun things together. You have to come back to reality sometimes. And then you are not going to be happy. Also, times with your friends are not always that great either. Things go wrong. There can be some friction, some disagreements. You don't always agree on everything, and that can bug you. You will need some time *away* from your friends in order to recover!

Friends are a good thing, in that they can make you happier for part of the time. But they cannot solve the eternal problem of how to be happier during the rest of your life… or for those moments when you wish that you were not with your friends right now!

5. Pursuing Power ♛

As it was with gaining things, gaining power may seem to bring you happiness for a while. But even this will fade and you will be having to pursue more power again in order to feel better. One trick the powerful may use to feel better for a moment is to exert their power in an abusive way. They could tell off a servant or subordinate in a nasty, petty way. This may make them feel that their power is really great and that they don't need any more. But this effect will not last. They will have to get on the treadmill again and work on getting another "power rush" to make them feel better… for a little while.

6. Fooling Yourself 😁

This seems like the magic trick. You fool yourself into thinking that you are happier than you really are. A lot of us do this. We like to think that we are better people than most other people, and that our ideas are much better ideas than they really are. But, deep down, we do not really believe our lies. We are unconsciously dissatisfied with what we are telling ourselves and secretly know that we are not the great people we would like to be and our ideas are not that perfect at all!

If only we could fool ourselves so successfully that our *subconscious* mind believed it then we could be happy, but it never works. Our subconscious always knows the truth.

7. Trying to Be Perfect 😇

If you can't fool yourself that you are really a better person then maybe you could try to become that person! That is the goal you could set so that you can finally feel better about yourself and your life. But do you think this goal is really achievable? Can a real human being ever be perfect? Unfortunately that goal is way out of reach for most of us! The closest we are ever likely to come to that goal is when we have successfully fooled ourselves. Only by fooling ourselves can we "become perfect".

An alternative would be to pat ourselves on the back for at least trying to be perfect. We may not be perfect beings yet, but at least we are making an effort! That's better than most people, right? But this will not make us feel better all the time because, let's face it, we have admitted that we are *not* perfect right now.

8. Keeping Busy ☹

If we can't make ourselves and our lives perfect then at least we could try to keep so busy that we don't notice this much of the time. This has some sense to it, because a busy mind is a distracted mind. If you don't have time to worry about your life then you *will not be worrying*.

What's wrong with this? Well, the fact that you are not actually feeling better means that when you do have to stop for a while you will remember that you are not happy. You can't be busy all the time, so there will be moments of dissatisfaction for you. And what about the subconscious mind? It will always be noticing that you are not happy, even during the times that you are keeping yourself busy. You need a better solution than this.

9. Following Your Dreams ✳

This is a solution that sounds like it could work. Except for the times when your dreams are going wrong. What if you are aiming for your goal and no matter what you do things keep going wrong? What if someone else gets to your goal ahead of you… and there are no openings left? Are you supposed to keep on trying anyway, no matter what? You could get exhausted aiming for a goal that you never achieve. Will that make you feel better?

This is where the idea of fooling yourself may come into play. Some "experts" recommend that you make yourself feel certain that a positive outcome must become available, as long as you "truly believe". Such nonsense may lead to a lot of bad feelings for yourself when the realities of this world relentlessly force themselves upon you.

10. Compromising ☹

Finally, let's look at compromising. This is the solution where you moderate your desires and lower your expectations so that you can be happy with something less than what you originally wanted. Sounds good?

The problem is that although compromised goals may be easier to achieve, they will always feel like something less. You might feel better than the way you would have if you hadn't compromised, but the "better" will be at a lower level. You will be *somewhat* happier, but also *somewhat dissatisfied*.

Still, this does point the way to a workable solution where you really can feel better.

WHAT DOES WORK ☺

What works is not to expect happiness from arranging a perfect life, getting things, attaching yourself to a special person, relying on your friends, pursuing power, fooling yourself, trying to be perfect, keeping busy, following your dreams or compromising. Instead you should rely on *being realistic*. What does this mean? I will explain it in the next chapters.

2. HOW TO REALISTICALLY IMPROVE YOUR FEELINGS

"Reality will make you happier."

The person who is the most realistic is the most happy. Why? Because it is the only thing that can really work. But why is that and how exactly can you do it?

THE SUBCONSCIOUS MIND 🏊

Your subconscious mind is bigger than your conscious mind. It works automatically beneath the surface. It is like the classic picture of an iceberg, where only a small tip is seen above the surface of the sea. This small tip is like the size of your conscious area. The enormous part beneath the surface is the huge area of your subconscious. You cannot see it, but it is there.

Much of what you do and think is actually determined by the subconscious area of your mind. If you take steps in the conscious area of your mind to make yourself happy, but you do not do anything about what is happening in the subconscious area, then you will still be unhappy. One way or another, your subconscious mind will take over and unsettle your feelings.

Some experts have advised that the subconscious is not intelligent and will believe anything that you tell it. They have said that all you need to do is repeat whatever you want your subconscious to believe, over and over, and eventually it will believe that this is the truth. It will then do whatever you needed it to do. Nothing could be further from the truth. The reality is that the subconscious mind is smart. It will realize that you have been trying to trick it and will generate responses that take this into account. Your repetition of untruths will come back to haunt you.

A better approach to take with your subconscious mind is to tell it the truth. Tell it that you want to feel better but you know that conditions are tough. Ask it if it can help with that. Is there any way to feel better in spite of how things are… a way that makes sense? Then see what it comes up with to help both of you: the conscious and the subconscious minds.

While you are waiting for a response you can do some more things with your conscious mind.

THE CONSCIOUS MIND 💡

The conscious mind may be small but it is not weak. It can do a lot. As long as the subconscious is on its side, it can help you to feel better. The trick is in how you use it.

As you know from experience, the conscious mind does not normally make you feel better. You could almost go so far as to say that the opposite is the case: most of the time the conscious mind makes you feel worse. Why is that? Because it is looking for things that go wrong and then trying to find if there is any way to fix them. Basically, that is how your conscious mind is designed. But you don't have to let it work in that manner. You can help it to help you!

The way to help your conscious mind is to ask it the right questions. For example, if it is remembering some terrible thing that happened to you in the past, you could ask it what good thing could be gained from that. And you mean: what realistic, sensible, genuinely-achievable good thing could be gained. You are not looking for anything that doesn't make sense here. You do not want answers that could not really work.

Some experts have written things like: "Whatever the mind of man (I assume this includes other types of people than men!) can conceive and believe, it can achieve" and "Understanding can overcome any situation, however mysterious or insurmountable it may appear to be." Well! Does that sound *realistic* to you? Better to ask your conscious mind for realistic solutions that could really work! Otherwise, how are you going to feel better when you struggle endlessly to achieve the impossible… or when you find that your "understanding" is not really great enough to overcome some stranger shooting at you on the street?

Okay. We've got that straight. We have to ask our conscious minds what realistic, sensible, genuinely-achievable good thing could be gained from that terrible memory from the past. At first it might say "nothing", but we will then just ask it again. "Are you sure there is nothing good that we can learn or gain from this?" And it might say to avoid these types of situations in the future... which is a good thing to learn.

But what if your conscious mind realizes that you cannot guarantee avoiding this terrible situation in the future? What then? You could ask it: "Is there absolutely nothing good that we can realistically gain from this?" And it might answer that at least you know what to look out for and try to avoid in the future. That is a good thing to know.

But let's not be too easy about this, as some experts have been. Let's examine this even further. What if this terrible memory from your past is something that you cannot seem to get away from? What if it is about your own intelligence, for example, or other abilities you lack? What are you supposed to do about that type of thing?

The experts may try to escape from this question by quoting some kind of "positive outlook" sort of thing, but I am not going to cheat you like that. I am saying you should be realistic, which means that you cannot escape from certain facts. Escaping is not the answer. You can feel better without hiding from the truth… and without trying any kind of "mental tricks".

If you want to feel better about some *permanent* lack of ability that you will never be able to get away from then you had better accept it and decide to learn to live with it, because it is not going to go away. You can resolve to take it as an absolute truth which you are not going to hide from yourself or anyone. After you have swallowed the bitter pill of this awful, inescapable truth then you can turn your back on it. It's not a secret anymore. You will be strangely empowered to overcome your worries about this and can move on with your life.

In a moment I will talk about ways to "move on with your life" which will help you to feel better, but first I will list some other "awful inescapable truths" that you might have to deal with.

SOME OTHER AWFUL INESCAPABLE TRUTHS 😱

<u>1. You Will Encounter People You Don't Like</u> 😕

It is an awful inescapable truth that you will meet people you don't like. Some of them may be people you encounter once. But some may be people you have to live with for years. Some will be at your workplace or at school. Some may be your own relatives, or even members of your immediate family! What are you supposed to do about this?

If you want to feel better then you had better accept this fact. This is how life is. If you try to deny it then you will most likely go crazy, because your subconscious mind won't like your denial. It wants action, not phony words! So swallow this bitter pill, accept the truth and decide that you will learn to live with it. You are not going to hide this from yourself.

And then what? Let's finish this short list of awful inescapable truths first and then I will give you some ideas about what you can do.

2. Some People Will Not Like You 😢

Just as you will not like some people, some people will not like you. This could be your fault, or it could be entirely theirs. It could be caused by something you did, or it could be caused by their narrow-minded prejudices, or some other weird thing about them. The reason doesn't matter. What matters is that whatever you do and whoever you are, *someone* will not like you. It's stupid and it's unfair but it is true.

Before you decide that you will try to make everyone like you, understand that this will never work. Even Jesus was disliked by some people! *Everyone* is disliked by someone. That is how it is.

Swallow this bitter pill – you will be a lot better off!

3. Bad Events Will Happen in the World

If not liking some people and not being liked by some other people was not awful enough, you also will have to face the existence of bad events happening in the world. Some of these will be remote and may not affect you personally, and others will directly impact your own life and those of your loved ones. That is reality. There will be wars, floods, fires, earthquakes, hurricanes, tornadoes, tsunamis, and so on. People will hate each other and fight each other. Nations will attack other nations. Rulers will cheat and oppress their people. That is how it is. Most times you will escape from the worst events in the world, but sometimes they will affect you. Lesser bad events will probably affect you quite often, such as inflation, poor leadership, social inequities, and so on. You might as well accept that there will always be something bad in the world that is affecting you and your loved ones.

4. Bad Events Will Happen in Your Life ☹

Apart from the bad events happening in the world, there will also be bad events happening in *your world*. Even if the world around you is going okay, things can still go wrong for you and your loved ones. I am sure that you have had enough bad experiences already to know that this is true!

5. You Will Get Sick ☹

One of the bad events that will happen in your life is that you will get sick… again. For most of us this may not have been too serious in the past, but some of us have had serious illnesses. Some of us are very sick right now. How are you supposed to feel better about your life when illness is either with you or looming on the horizon? And it's not just a prospect for yourself, it is also a prospect for your loved ones. This is another bitter pill of an awful inescapable truth that you are going to have to swallow!

6. Accidents Will Happen 😮

Things will go wrong. Accidents will happen. They could be trivial, like spilling the milk, or they could be major – which I don't want to describe! If I start to list all the accidents that could happen to you and your loved ones then I am afraid I will become very boring and annoying to you. I think you can easily imagine all these things. No doubt some have already happened in your life. They have certainly happened to me!

7. You Will Get Older 🕐

No matter what you do to avoid it, you will get older. Hopefully. You can look after your health, eat right, exercise, avoid too much sun, but you will still age. There is no getting around it. When you were very young, getting older seemed like a good thing. But now you are mature it looks like a downhill journey!

8. Your Time on Earth Will Expire ☹

At the end of it all, you will end. None of us knows when it will be, thank heavens, but we all know it is going to come one day. Some of us know that we are closer to this day, as I do. Some think it is far away. Let's hope that's right.

9. You Will Make Mistakes ☹

No one gets everything right. Everyone gets something wrong. It is inevitable that you will make some more mistakes in your life, as you have done before. Sometimes you will think that you should have known better, and sometimes you *couldn't* have known any better. Whatever the reason, you will still get something wrong sometime in the future.

10. You Probably Will Not Achieve All of Your Dreams 😰

A lot of well-meaning people tell us to pursue our dreams. They want us to feel fulfilled and good about our lives. They rightly say that unless we chase after our dreams then we may never achieve them. But, what if we chase after our dreams and for some reason we don't achieve some of them? What if, heaven forbid, we don't achieve any of them? Then how will we feel? Perhaps like we wasted our time?

There are *no guarantees* in life, except maybe that some things will go wrong! You have to face this possibility: you may not achieve any of your dreams, no matter what you do, and you almost certainly will never achieve *all* of them. That doesn't mean that you shouldn't chase after them. But it does mean that you should be realistic about the possible outcomes.

WHAT TO DO ABOUT THE AWFUL INESCAPABLE TRUTHS 😊

How can you feel better about the inevitable and inescapable awful truths that are going to upset your life? At first it might seem wise to forget about them. Better to fool yourself and take an optimistic view. Maybe it won't happen to you. But the trouble with this is that your subconscious won't believe you and it will come back to haunt you. It will make you regret this: "That way madness lies".

Rather than trying to cheat your subconscious and escape from these awful truths, you should face up to them and accept them as they are. Only then will you be empowered to truly overcome their negative impact on your feelings. Only then can you move on with your life and make yourself feel better.

How can you move on from these awful facts?

MOVING ON FROM THE AWFUL INESCAPABLE TRUTHS 🏃

One interesting fact about the awful inescapable truths is that they have a better side. I am not saying that there is a wonderful opposite side to them, at least not all the time. But I am saying that there are moderate and sometimes even very good sides to them. Let's list some of these.

1. You May Have a Permanent Lack of Some Abilities ☹

This was the first thing we discussed. But it has a better side:

1. You Will Have Some Abilities ☺

Yes, that's right. You may lack some abilities that you wish you had, or would have liked to have had, but you will also always have some abilities. Maybe these will not be at the top of the whole world, or maybe, rarely, they will be. But they will certainly exist. Everyone has some abilities. This is a good thing and you should consciously remind yourself about it so that you can feel better about your life. It is also worth reminding your subconscious about this fact too, so that it can come to the party. 🎉

2. You Will Encounter People You Don't Like 😒

This is the second thing we discussed. But it has a better side:

2. You Will Encounter People You Do Like 😊 (and also some you can tolerate ☺)

Not only will you inevitably encounter people you don't like, you will also inevitably encounter people you *do* like. And you will encounter a lot of people whom you don't mind at all. This is good news. It's worth reminding yourself about this when you are encountering or thinking about the people you don't like in your life. There are other kinds of people who make life worth living! And plenty who are not a problem to you and me. Not everything is bad.

3. Some People Will Not Like You 😖

The better side of this is, obviously:

3. Some People Will Like You 😃 (and some will not mind you ☺)

It is inevitable that some people will like you, even if you are not sure why! Even the worst people are liked by someone, (which is one of those strange things in life). But you are not even remotely the worst of people, so plenty of people will like you. That is reality.

Plenty of other people may not like you all that much, but they won't mind you. You will get no trouble from them. Most of us can get on with just about everyone. It is only those really terrible people that most of us have trouble with. The rest of us are fine and okay to get on with. That is another fact about human beings. You can rely on that.

When you are remembering someone who didn't like you, take some time out to remember the ones who did like you. It will put things into perspective.

4. Bad Events Will Happen in the World

The better side:

4. Good Events Will Happen in the World
(and plenty of ordinary events)

Yes, even though plenty of bad events will happen in the world, there will also be plenty of good events! This is a fact. There will be peace, good weather, international cooperation, safety and security, sunny days, bumper harvests, and so on. People will like each other and help each other. Nations will trade with and assist each other. Rulers will (sometimes) support and promote the welfare of their people.

Apart from the good events, there will be many, many ordinary events. The days of the world are filled with ordinary events… which is a lot better than having bad events happen! You do not need to be dismayed by the large number of ordinary events that happen: this is a good thing. Remember that and enjoy this fact, as although we may not be having as many good events as we would like, at least we are not always being overwhelmed by bad ones!

5. Bad Events Will Happen in Your Life 😟

The better side, obviously:

5. Good Events Will Happen in Your Life 😊

Yes, it's true: good events will occur for you! No matter what is going on in the world, good events can and will occur in your world. Think back across your life to see if this is true. You are sure to find good events that happened to you and your loved ones.

Our minds are tuned in to looking at problems, which can make us forget all the good things that we have experienced. Nature thinks that good things don't need much thought, as those things cannot hurt us. But if we take a moment to remember the good things then we will feel so much better!

6. You Will Get Sick 🙁

The better side to this is:

6. You Will Usually Recover 🙂

Most times when you get sick you will recover and be healthy again. In fact, for most of our lives most of us are in good health. Maybe our health could be better, that part is often up to us, but in general it's not too bad. This is not to make light of the fact that sometimes we will not recover, or we will suffer from the long-term consequences of our illnesses. But it is to say that we should remind ourselves to be grateful for the times when we do recover and are in good health.

For those of us who have long-term health issues, which includes me and some of my loved ones, we can still be grateful for the better days and the fact that there is some time left for us on earth. Being alive is a blessing in itself, which is worth remembering.

7. Accidents Will Happen 😲

But the better side is:

7. Things Will Often Go Right... Or, at Least, Okay 👌

Sometimes things will go wrong. But most of the time they will go right, or, in the worst case, they will go okay. Most times you will not spill the milk, crash the car, trip over and hurt yourself, and so on. Most of the things you do will turn out the way you intended. Also, many of the things that do go wrong will be easy to fix. If you burn the toast you can scrape it off, or make a new batch. If you trip you will usually be able to avoid injuring yourself. If you cut yourself you will usually be able to disinfect the wound and put on a Band-Aid or plaster. Rarely you will need stitches, which you can boast about later. Most accidents are minor accidents.

I don't want to be unrealistic here and make light of the accidents that will happen. But I do want to remind you that most of the time things will not go wrong. And even when they do go wrong, most of the time they will not go seriously wrong. You will be able to fix them, or even ignore them and move on. These are good points to keep in mind – they will help you to feel better about your life.

8. You Will Get Older 🕐

The better side is:

8. You Are Still Alive! 🙌

Not only are you still alive, you have lived. That is an amazing gift. If you are older then you have had many years of living. Not everyone gets to have that. Count yourself lucky. If you are younger then most likely you will have many years of living ahead. Some of those times are sure to be interesting, enjoyable and worthwhile. Look forward to that. Being alive is a wonderful thing, even if it is not all plain sailing!

9. Your Time on Earth Will Expire ☹

But, on the better side:

9. Your Time Has Not Expired Yet! 😎

However long you've got left, it is not over yet! Be grateful for the time that is granted to you to stay on the Earth. Use it well.

10. You Will Make Mistakes 😕

On the better side:

10. You Will Get Many Things Right ☺

No one gets everything right, but in spite of the mistakes that you will inevitably make in your life, most of what you do will turn out well. Or at least well enough!

Even when you get something wrong, you will usually be able to learn from it. You can do it better next time. You can improve. Mistakes are also opportunities.

The truth is that nobody's perfect, including you. The real problem is not when people make mistakes, it's when they fail to learn from them. This doesn't have to be you. You can *gain* from your errors.

11. You Probably Will Not Achieve All of Your Dreams 😨

The better side of this is:

11. You Will Achieve Something 🏆

Maybe you won't score the gold medal, but you will achieve some things in your life. If you pursue your dreams, or at least make an effort, then you will get somewhere. You will gain some skill, make some money, maybe buy some kind of property, all sorts of things. Even if you don't achieve all of your dreams, maybe you will achieve some of them. Or it may be that you don't get to the absolute top, but at least you are part way up the mountain. Being part way up looks better than never having tried to do anything and remaining at the bottom.

There is a pattern to all of the things that I have just told you. It is that after you have faced up to the awful inescapable truths about life you can then move on to look at the better side. And when you look at the better side you will often *feel* better. This gives us a key to finding other ways to feel better.

3. OTHER REALISTIC WAYS TO FEEL BETTER

"There are many realistic ways to feel better."

As I said before, our minds were designed by nature to look for problems and then to try to solve them. This makes sense, because we had to survive. If human beings hadn't survived then we wouldn't be having this discussion right now!

The big problem with this is that we can spend so much time on problems that we start to feel bad. Then we keep feeling bad for most of our lives. But it doesn't have to be like this. We can do something about it.

The first thing we can do is to admit that not all of our problems can be solved all of the time. Things will go wrong, no matter what we do. We have to be realistic about this so that we can then move on.

After that, we can work out what we *can* do. We have some power to fix some of the things in our lives. We also have some power to improve things. The fixing and improving that we can do will help us to feel better about those things.

Finally, we can learn to look at the better side, in an entirely realistic way. We have to be realistic because our subconscious will not buy it if we try to fool it. It will come back to haunt us if we try to be too clever with it.

Let's apply these steps to the areas we have already looked at.

1. You May Have a Permanent Lack of Some Abilities ☹

First, we must admit that we may never have some of the abilities we wish we had. This could be a problem that we can never solve. We may be able to find a way around some of these deficiencies, but we may never gain all the abilities we desire. Sad, horrible, but true.

Second, we should work out what we *can* do. We may be able to fix some of the issues. Also, we may actually have some level of abilities that we can put to good use. Maybe we can even *improve* our abilities in some way. For example, we may not be the best-looking person in the world, but we can choose clothes and styles that make us look better. Another example, we could improve the abilities we do have by training, practice and education.

Finally, we should make an effort to look – realistically – on the better side: "1. You Will Have Some Abilities ☺ ". Remember that? Not everything is bad. And you may be able to use some of those abilities to make up for the ones you don't have. I don't mean that they can always *replace* what you lack, but at least they are something that you *can* benefit from. The most important thing here is to concentrate on the good side of your life. You want to balance the bad side with the good, so that you don't forget that you have it. The bad will no longer be able to overwhelm you with its negativity. You can feel better in a realistic way, because this is the truth. You have some abilities and these should not be ignored just because you may lack some others. It's not *all* bad. And this will make you feel better.

Let's just take a quick look at the sort of things that you can do with your actual abilities in order to make up for the ones you may lack. If you lack perfect looks, (doesn't that apply to most of us?), then you can use your other abilities to make your life work. Maybe you are good at sport – can you make that into a career? If not, then are you good enough to join an amateur team where you can make friends and enjoy yourself? You might as well get some pleasure out of your ability! Maybe you are good at more intellectual pursuits. Can you make a career out of those? If not, then can you enjoy intellectual pursuits in your spare time? Do you have skills in craft? Can you use those to benefit yourself in some way, even if it is just for enjoyment? Artistic abilities? Can you do something with those? People are not valuable only when they have perfect looks. There are other things that can make them valuable, such as their sport, intellectual, craft, artistic, and other abilities. You can be "attractive" through other things than your looks.

What if you are a quadriplegic? You could search through your other abilities to see what you can do. Maybe you are good at creating stories, academic work, counseling… there are many areas where you could develop and use the abilities you have.

The point of all this is that the alternative is to continue to feel bad about what you lack. If you want to feel better then this second step of working out what you *can* do should definitely be on your agenda!

Moving on to the next item:

2. You Will Encounter People You Don't Like ☹

First, we must admit that this is always going to happen. There is no way around it. We will *always* meet people we don't like. Even if we go and live up on a mountain, someone will turn up one day and ruin everything. Anyway, who wants to live up on a mountain by themselves? Not me! So, we had better admit that meeting unlikable people is going to *have to* happen to us.

Second, we should work out what we can do about this problem. We can't fix all the people we may meet in our lives, but we can "fix" some things about ourselves. What things? The way we react, for one. And the way we deal with unlikable people, for another. And, also, the way we view ourselves in relation to other people. How important are they compared to us?

How do we "fix" the way we react? Well, if we want to feel better then why do we react so strongly to some of the people we don't like? Our strong dislike and even hatred of some people drives us to feel really bad. This comes from our ancient design as creatures which needed to survive. Hatred can generate adrenaline, which fires up our bodies so that we can fight. Forgetting about the risk to ourselves, we grow stronger and stronger in our desire to attack and destroy the people we hate. In earlier times this could lead to fighting and even murder and wars. But none of this makes us feel better!

If we understand what this is all about – our ancient human design – then we can take a step back and say: "It is smarter to calm down and find sensible solutions to the existence of people we don't like so that we can safely feel better each day of our lives."

How can we improve the way we deal with unlikable people? By being realistic. It is realistic to check what level of damage the other person could cause to you and your loved ones. Knowing that, you can then decide if any action is actually needed. In many cases the other person cannot (or would not want to) do any real damage, so no actual action is needed. You can ignore them. In some cases the damage can be easily avoided by you, so only simple action is needed. An example would be where someone cuts you off in traffic. You only need to slow down to avoid an accident. You do not need to chase after them and try to smash your car into theirs! Lastly, in some cases the person could cause serious damage to you and your loved ones. In those cases you need to think carefully about how you can protect yourselves. The easiest and most effective action is what you should be looking for. For example, you could call the police, or consult a lawyer, or get out of that place! I'm sure you know these things already.

How can we "fix" the way we view ourselves in relation to other people? How can we improve our view of how important they are compared to us? When we see ourselves as more important than other people then we worry about them less. They may be unlikable, but this has less impact on our feelings. When we see the unlikable people as more important than ourselves then we feel worse about them. We can fix this by remembering what makes a person truly important in the world. True importance is not when a person has worldly power, riches, or even great abilities. True importance is when a person brings benefits to the world. When we remember this then we will feel better about the unlikable people who are merely powerful, rich or talented.

The other problem with unlikable people who are "above us" in the world is when they can use their power against us. How can you fix that? One way is via the political approach. One political answer is to seek more power for yourself so that you get above the troublesome person. Then you can tell *them* what to do! Another political answer is to join a political party, or start a new one, or vote for one that will stop the troublesome person. Another (nasty) political answer is to undermine the powerful person by spreading rumors, gossiping, and so on. You could also use "passive resistance", where you peacefully disobey the orders of the powerful person. But, you may not want to make the effort involved in any of these political approaches. And, I think, they probably will not make you feel any better!

A second way to fix the problem of unlikable people using their power against you is to avoid them whenever you can. If you can get away from them then do it! After that you should try to forget about them, as every time you think about them you will feel worse. Better to forget that they ever existed. If you can't get away from them then you should keep reminding yourself that they are not truly important people. They are merely more powerful, richer, or have some better ability than you... at the moment. But they are still *unlikable people*, which means that they definitely are not truly important. Truly important people *are always likable*.

The last step we should take is to make an effort to look realistically on the better side: "2. You Will Encounter People You Do Like 😊 (and also some you can tolerate 🙂)". Thank heavens that this is the case! Keep this in mind when encountering the unlikable kind of people. Balance the bad by remembering the good.

The next item:

3. Some People Will Not Like You 😖

First, we must admit that this is always going to happen, no matter what we do. Even if you were the smartest, nicest, most attractive person in the world, *someone* would not like you. You will never be able to change this. Accept this fact, and move on.

Second, we should work out what we can do about this problem. We *can* fix and improve ourselves in this area. Manners, appearance, attitude towards others: these can all be improved. Good manners – the most appropriate for the people you are with – will make you more likable. Improving your appearance could make you more likable. The trick is to know which type of appearance will appeal to the people you meet. Unfortunately you will never be able to appeal to everyone, but you can aim to look right for the people you want to associate with! Your attitude towards others may also be able to be improved. Generally, people like people who like and respect them. Bear that in mind when you are talking to them!

Finally, as always, we should make an effort to look realistically on the better side: "3. Some People Will Like You 😁 (and some will not mind you ☺)". That's good news, isn't it? Remember all the people who liked you and I bet they outnumber the ones you had trouble with – right? Keep things in perspective and you are sure to feel better.

Next:

4. Bad Events Will Happen in the World
⚡ 🌋 🔥 💧 💣 🔪

Of course they will. They always do. Let's accept this fact and move on.

Second, what can we do about this problem? Truthfully, usually very little. Otherwise, why would we have all these problems today? Wouldn't we have put an end to them if we could? But what we can do is the little things. We can aim for peace, put out fires, build levees to protect from floods, evacuate people before hurricanes hit, promote democracy, vote for better leaders, and so on. If you carry out even one small helpful action then you will definitely feel better in yourself. And by working together, the people of the world will eventually fix as many of these problems as we can.

Finally, looking realistically on the better side we have to admit: "4. Good Events Will Happen in the World ☀ ⛰ ☃ 🍃 💌 ☮ (and plenty of ordinary events ⛅ 🌙 🌱 ⏰ 🛁 👫 🚙 🚌 🔨 📱 🍽 🚶 💤)". Remember this fact… and feel better about it all!

Next up:

5. Bad Events Will Happen in Your Life 😦

Obviously. They already have, and there are probably more to come. Swallow this bitter pill.

Second, is there anything we can do about this? Certainly, there is a lot we can do. We can prepare for the future. We can consider what might go wrong and do something about it today. We can improve ourselves and our situation. These are not magic fixes, but they are workable ones. We won't be able to avoid every bad event, but we will be able to avoid some of them, and we will also be able to reduce the impact of the ones that still get through.

Finally, we remind ourselves that: "5. Good Events Will Happen in Your Life ☺". Actively remembering the ones that have already happened will make us feel better.

6. You Will Get Sick ☹

As has happened to you before, you will get sick again. I wish that this was not the case for you, but I do not have the power to stop it! I would if I could. Unfortunately you had better get used to this idea. Please swallow this bitter pill. You will be better off.

Second, there are things that you can do about you and your family getting sick. I am sure that you have already heard about these: eating well, keeping reasonably fit, getting enough sleep, reducing stress, having regular medical checkups, not smoking, and so on. All of these will help you to reduce your chances of getting sick. And they may also help to reduce the severity of your illnesses when you do get sick. If you do these helpful things then you will feel better about the way you are taking care of yourself and your family. If you choose not to do them then your subconscious will be upset and will torment you in various sneaky ways – because it wants you to survive!

When you do get sick then you can help yourself in several ways. Avoiding a visit to the doctor when you are not sure if something is serious is not a good one! It is better to find out earlier if something is seriously wrong. The medical profession will have more chance of helping you then. But if your illness does not seem serious, such as a cold, then getting rest and plenty of fluids will help you to recover more quickly. If you can arrange to do this then so much the better.

Finally, you can remind yourself when you are sick that: "6. You Will Usually Recover ☺". Be grateful that this will usually be the case. For the times when it turns out that you have long-term health issues, remind yourself that some days will be better than others and try to be grateful that there is some time left for you on the Earth. I am with you on this one!

7. Accidents Will Happen 😮

As you know, accidents will happen. Mostly they will be minor ones, but there is the possibility of a major one happening one day. Let's hope not. But we must accept that there is that possibility. This acceptance will let us move on with our lives.

Second, there are things we can do to reduce the possibility of accidents happening to us. We can also take steps to reduce the impact of any future accidents if they do occur. For example, we could take out insurance. Another example would be to set aside some money in a nest egg which could help us deal with future mishaps.

There are many ways that we could reduce the chances of accidents happening in our lives, including: learning defensive driving, installing safety devices in our homes and workplaces, getting a good night's rest... all sorts of things! If you have taken some of these steps then you will be feeling much better about your future.

Finally: "7. Things Will Often Go Right... Or, at Least, Okay 🐾". This is worth remembering, especially when you find yourself worrying about the future. It's not *always* going to go wrong. Generally things turn out the way we intended... or, at least, in an okay kind of way. (And many of the things that don't go right will be easy enough to fix.) You can feel better about all that!

8. You Will Get Older 🕐

This is obvious. Some of us think about this a lot! Especially those of us who are "over the hill" of middle age. For us this problem is easier to admit! So, let's admit it will happen and move on.

Second, there are things we can do to improve our longevity. These are all obvious. They are the same as the ones I mentioned for reducing the times we get sick. And we should add to that the things we do to reduce the chances of accidents happening to us. That's all good. But, so far, there is no permanent solution to the problem of aging! Sorry about that.

Finally, you really should remind yourself that: "8. You Are Still Alive! 🙌 ". It certainly is a good thing to have: life! Be thankful for the days you have had and look forward to the ones to come. Balance the bad side of the truth with the good.

9. Your Time on Earth Will Expire ☹

It certainly will. We don't know when it will be, but it will come. Let's admit that fact and move on.

Second, we can do all the things I mentioned before to improve our lifespan. There are no guarantees, but we can at least reduce the risk of our lives ending earlier than they should have. This might also be a good time to think about what legacy we will leave. How will we be remembered? Will it be well or badly? We may feel better today if we can honestly say that we were happy with how we have conducted our lives. We have not been perfect, no one has, but we did our best to live well and leave the world a little better than how we found it.

Finally, we can remember that: "9. Our Time Has Not Expired Yet! 😎". Isn't that a good thing? And it gives us the opportunity to do some more living, and to work on leaving that good legacy that has meaning for us!

10. You Will Make Mistakes 😳

Inevitably you will. It can't be helped – at least, not completely. Accept that you will get some things wrong some day in the future… and move on from that fact.

Second, we can learn from our errors. If we make it our habit to learn what we can from the things that we got wrong then we definitely can gain from these and do better in the future. Being sad, ashamed or depressed about the errors we have made will not bring us any benefit. But we *can* benefit if we choose to learn from them.

Finally, it is also true that: "10. You Will Get Many Things Right ☺". Of course you will. Most of what you do will turn out the way you intended. Otherwise everyone would have to stay at home and be careful not to do anything while they were there! It's not like that. Most of the things that we do work out well. Or, at least well enough! Enjoy that fact, and feel better.

11. You Probably Will Not Achieve All of Your Dreams 😰

You may choose to pursue your dreams, but that doesn't mean that all of them will come true. You will, most likely, achieve something if you make the effort to pursue your dreams. You will make some improvements and get somewhere. But there is no guarantee that you will get to the top, or achieve *exactly* what you dreamt of. Accept that this could be the outcome, and move on.

Second, we *can* improve our chances of getting somewhere on the journey towards our dreams. "Dedication" is the word that can help us here. We need to be dedicated in our approach to achieving our dreams. This does not mean that we need to be unrealistic. It just means that we should be dedicated! If we are not dedicated to our goals then we won't get far.

If you find that you are having difficulty dedicating yourself to one of your dreams then this is telling you something. It may not be telling you that you are lazy or lacking in self-control. More likely it is telling you that this is *not really one of your dreams*. It may be time to stop and choose a dream that you are genuinely interested in.

Finally, when we have not reached our dreams we can remind ourselves that: "11. You Will Achieve Something 🏆". If we make the effort to pursue our dreams then we will get somewhere. This looks better than if we never tried to do anything in our lives.

The pattern we have been discussing in the above examples can be applied to anything. If we want to feel better about something we can consciously:

1. Admit that some bad things will always happen no matter what we do… and then move on from this point. 🗑

2. Fix or improve what we can, where we can… when it is worth the effort to us. 🔨

3. Look at the genuine good side… realistically balance the bad with the good. ☃

We can feel better by applying these points via our conscious mind, but what can we do to help our subconscious mind?

4. THE SUBCONSCIOUS

"Happier subconscious, happier you."

The subconscious is that huge area of your mind beneath the surface. It cannot be seen by your conscious mind, but it is there. It determines much of what you think and do. How can you work with it to feel better?

First, what is your subconscious? Your subconscious is like an ancient animal which has developed over billions of years. It has one idea: "Help me and my kind to survive!" It creates feelings, thoughts and actions to achieve this. Sometimes your conscious mind is aware of some part of the feelings and thoughts. Also, you can see some of the actions, but others are not seen. You don't see the regulation of your internal body temperature, the movements of your digestive system, and so on. You see reflex actions *after* they have occurred. You normally do not notice your breathing. All this is done by your subconscious to keep "your animal part" alive.

What does this mean for how you feel? The subconscious creates its own feelings and thoughts. Some of these get through to your conscious mind. If the subconscious is feeling bad then, most probably, your conscious mind will start to feel bad. If the subconscious comes up with a negative thought then some part of that will come through to your conscious mind, making it have negative thoughts. If you want to feel better then you will have to make your subconscious feel better too!

How can you make your subconscious feel better? By giving it what it wants. Your subconscious wants you to "help it and its kind to survive". In other words, it wants to be safe and to flourish. And it wants similar people to yourself to also be safe and to flourish. You can give it this... well, as much as is realistically possible!

"Being safe and flourishing" is another way of saying that you won the lottery and can do anything that you wish. You never have to work again. You don't have to worry about the roof over your head, where your next meal is coming from, what the boss thinks of you... you can go anywhere and do anything. But this is not likely to happen. So what can you do for your subconscious instead?

You can keep its stomach full, give it a safe place to sleep, arrange fun activities for it, and generally look after its "animal-style" interests. Treat it like a favorite pet which you want to look after. What does that pet need? Food, shelter, comfort, safety, leadership, companionship, fun, and so on. Arrange all these things for your subconscious self. This will make it feel better, and it will then generate more positive feelings and thoughts to pass on to you. A contented subconscious means a happier conscious mind.

Let's look at this in more detail. What should you do to make your subconscious more contented? What should you avoid doing?

DOS AND DON'TS WITH YOUR SUBCONSCIOUS 🙊 🙊 🙊 🙊

1. For Its Stomach 🍽

DO… feed it when it is hungry. This will make it feel satisfied. ☺
DON'T… fill it up with junk food. This will make it sick. ☹

2. For Its Shelter 🏠

DO… find it a good place to live. This will make it feel at home. ☺
DON'T… compete to get it the best house ever. This will make it stressed. 😬

3. For Its Comfort 🛋

DO… give it good furniture to rest on. This will make it feel at ease. ☺
DON'T… avoid all exercise. This will make it unhealthy. ☹

4. For Its Safety ☂

DO… take care of your finances. This will make it feel secure. ☺
DON'T… struggle to become rich. This will make it worry. ☹

5. For Its Leadership 🚶‍♂️

DO... guide it in the best things to do. This will make it feel protected. ☺
DON'T... indulge its every whim. This will make it reckless. It will end in tears. 😢

6. For Its Companionship 🙋

DO... introduce it to good friends. This will make it feel accepted. ☺
DON'T... let it mix with just anyone. This will put it in danger. 😱

7. For Its Activities 🚶

DO... involve it in good, healthy fun. This will make it feel engaged in life. 😄
DON'T... allow it to get involved in everything it wants... or to do nothing at all. This will make it rot... ☹ ...or end up being filled with regrets. 😟

Look after your subconscious and its desires. But in a responsible, adult way. Then it will feel safe and protected. It will be feeling better and will pass this on to you.

But, realistically, how much of this is possible? What about the times when it goes wrong? How can you help your subconscious to feel better then?

LEADING YOUR SUBCONSCIOUS 🚶

As we discussed, when things go wrong our conscious mind should admit that some bad things will always happen no matter what we do… and then move on from this point. But our subconscious is like an ancient animal which has developed over billions of years. It only has the one idea: "Help me and my kind to survive!" When things go wrong it will not be able to accept them and move on. It will want answers. It will want to know what can be done to reverse the situation so that things *only go right*. How can we feel better when that is happening in our minds?

The answer is to understand that the subconscious really is like an ancient animal. It is smart, but not in the same way that we are smart. It is not able to control itself in the way that we can. It cannot see life from a wider point of view, as we do. But we can lead it. We can take it by the hand and show it the way to a better view of our lives via the following three steps:

1. Answer Its Needs 👤

The subconscious has its needs. If we ignore them it will become distressed. It will feed bad feelings to our conscious mind. It will also try to take over by sending us frantic thoughts about the issues that are being ignored. We could accept these thoughts and start to act on them. But if we instead start by aiming to answer the needs of our subconscious then it will not get so distressed. It will see that we are trying to help it. It will then wait to see if our solutions really work. If they work then our subconscious will change its focus to its other needs, if any are coming to its attention.

But what if we cannot answer its needs this time because there is no workable way to do it?

2. Redirect Its Attention ☞

When there is no realistic solution to a problem then we have to accept it. Our subconscious will not like that and will make a fuss. But our subconscious is also tuned in to what is happening right now. If we redirect its attention to another matter then it may switch its focus onto that. It is like guiding a small child. If the child's problem is not forcing itself to their attention then we can often get them to think about something else. The same applies to the subconscious. If the problem is not forcing itself to its attention then we, the more adult part of the mind, can consciously redirect the subconscious onto another matter. If we are wise we will choose a less distressing one!

Redirecting the attention can be done in a similar way to what we did with the conscious mind. We can use the same three steps:

1. Admit that this bad thing has happened but there is nothing we can think of to fix it right now. We are stuck with it and will have to move on. 😐 🚮

2. If we could we would fix or improve on this, but we can't think of anything at this stage. Maybe we will think of something later, but right now we will have to find a way to live with what has happened. 🔨

3. The truth is that although we really do have this problem, not everything is bad and some things in our lives are even quite good. Let's redirect our focus to those and the things we can fix or improve. ☞ ⛄

3. Look for Better Answers 🔎

Finally, we should commit to finding better answers to meet the needs of our subconscious in the future. If we keep looking for ways to fix and improve then our subconscious will see that we are on its side. We really want the best for it. We are clearly the most trustworthy of leaders and it will want to follow us towards the better future. Maybe the future won't be perfect, obviously, but at least our heart will always be in the right place!

Our subconscious will feel better about that.

GETTING ANSWERS FROM OUR SUBCONSCIOUS 🧘

Earlier in the book we asked our subconscious mind if it could help us to feel better in spite of the way things are... a way that makes sense. We were waiting for its response. The reason we asked is that the subconscious has the ability to think. This goes on without us being aware of it, except that occasionally an answer "pops into our head". The subconscious has told us the answer that it has come up with after thinking about it for a while. This means that we *can* ask it for ways to help us feel better!

Some experts have said that the subconscious is like a supercomputer which can solve any problem we give it. We only have to clearly visualize what we want and the subconscious will get to work and eventually give us the perfect answer. If that were true then why are there so many problems still happening in the world today? It's just one of those unrealistic exaggerations again! But, the subconscious does have some ability to think on its own and there is no reason why you shouldn't work with that. You can check the usefulness of the answers it comes up with yourself. You have that ability, as you are the adult part of your mind.

WHAT KIND OF ANSWERS MIGHT THE SUBCONSCIOUS GIVE?

The subconscious will give a range of answers, from the silly through to the brilliant. An example of the silly would be it saying that you should eat a lot of chocolate in order to feel good. You know better than that! An example of the brilliant would be when it says that you should do something worthwhile with your life in order to feel fulfilled. That probably makes a lot of sense... once you work out what the worthwhile thing would be exactly, whether it would really work for you, and whether you would truly enjoy that kind of life.

Still, it is a good idea to ask your subconscious for its thoughts on how to feel better and then take a look at what it comes up with. You can use your conscious, adult-style judgment to decide which ones you really want to run with. Also, the subconscious will see that you are interested in its needs and are listening to it. This will make it feel better, which it will pass on to you. And, you never know, some of its ideas could turn out to be really important in your life!

WHAT DOES THE SUBCONSCIOUS WANT FOR OTHER PEOPLE? 👥

The subconscious does not just think about itself. Its idea is to "Help me and *my kind* to survive!" What does it mean by "my kind"? It means anyone or anything which it sees as being in the same group as itself. But who is that?

The obvious would be its family, because "blood is thicker than water". Then it may include people of its nationality. Or maybe only certain people in its country. It may add those of the same religious view. Or similar educational background. Or… whatever! The truth is that it automatically works these things out based on its ancient animal nature. Speaking of animals, the subconscious may include its pets as members of its family. These lucky pets will then be treated as members of "my kind". They will be protected under the umbrella of those it wants to help to survive.

If you want your subconscious to feel better, you will need to include the safety and flourishing of its imagined "group members" in your plans.

DOS WITH YOUR SUBCONSCIOUS FOR ITS GROUP 🐵

1. For Its Group's Stomachs 🍽 🍽 🍽

DO… feed the closest of them when they are hungry. Support the principle of the feeding of all of them, however that would actually be achieved! This will make your subconscious feel that it is considerate. 😇

2. For Its Group's Shelters 🏠 🏠 🏠

DO… find the closest of them good places to live. Support the principle that all of them should be well-housed. This will make your subconscious feel that it has protected its friends. 😌

3. For Its Group's Comfort 👑 👑 👑

DO… give the closest of them good furniture to rest on. Support the principle that all of them should be comfortable. This will make your subconscious feel that it is thoughtful. ☺

4. For Its Group's Safety ☂ ☂ ☂

DO… take care of your finances to cover at least the closest of the group. Support the principle that all of them should be financially secure. This will make your subconscious feel that it is caring. ☺

5. For Its Group's Leadership 👥

DO… if your position within the group allows it, guide the closest of them in the best things to do. Support the principle that good leadership should take care of all the group's members. This will make your subconscious feel that it is being reasonable. 😐

6. For Its Group's Companionship 🙋 🙋 🙋

DO… introduce the closest of them to your good friends. Support the principle that all members of the group should be able to find good companionship. This will make your subconscious feel that it is likable. ☺

7. For Its Group's Activities 大 大 大

DO… join the closest of them in good, healthy fun. Support the principle that good, healthy fun should be available to all members of the group. This will make your subconscious feel that it is engaged in the group. ☺

As the adult part of your mind, you may question which groups and which group members are really worth supporting. But if you want to feel better you will have to support some of your subconscious's ideas about who is "my kind". This is another area where you may want to lead your subconscious towards a better understanding of who should really be supported in our world. Answer its needs, so that you can feel better, but guide it as well!

Let's take a look at how we can feel better about those "other people" in the next chapter.

5. OTHER PEOPLE

"Some people are a huge challenge to our feeling better, but we can find a way."

Other people have a big impact on how we feel. Sometimes they make us feel terrible. How can we feel better when that happens?

The reality is that some people are really horrible. Any view about people which ignores this fact is not covering all of the truth. Even if it is only a minority which does horrible things, that minority still exists. This means that if we want to feel better then we have to know how we can achieve this even when we see horrible people and the horrible things they do. It is a big challenge!

If that wasn't bad enough, even ordinary people can do horrible things sometimes.

We notice this especially when they are following a horrible leader. The ordinary people under a horrible leader can get involved in all sorts of nightmarish activities. Think of the wars, the racism, the sexism, and all those kinds of things! What can we do to feel better when all of these are happening?

We have already discussed some of the solutions to this problem:

1. Swallow the bitter pill that this is how the world really is.

2. Calm down and find sensible solutions to the existence of horrible people so that we can safely feel better each day of our lives.

3. Check what level of damage the horrible person can actually cause to us and our loved ones to see if any action is genuinely needed.

4. If action is needed, look for the easiest and most effective ones, such as getting out of that place or calling the police.

5. Avoid horrible people and their followers whenever we can and put them out of our minds, as if they never existed.

6. Remind ourselves that horrible people are not truly important as they are unlikable. Truly important people *are always likable*.

7. Remind ourselves that not everyone in the world is a horrible person. Balance the bad with the good.

8. For the things we can't overcome today, commit ourselves to trying to find better answers in the future… if we can!

All this is good, but is it enough? What can we do to realistically feel better when the worst things are happening to us and the people we value, and we cannot find any way to stop them? If we can answer that then we will have a solution for all the bad times.

The answer is: "It is better to light a candle than to curse the darkness." Have you heard that before? But what candle, against what darkness, and what does it mean to light it?

The darkness is the horrible people and the horrible things that they and their followers may do to us and people like us. Cursing them will not make us feel better.

The candle is a genuine solution which can work in a small area around us. It cannot overcome the darkness, but it can light the area where we are located. The darkness has not been overcome, but it is no longer important here.

What is it to light the candle? We have to take action to find and light the candle before it will start working for us. After we light the candle it will take care of itself, for as long as it can last. We can relax and enjoy its benefit, even if this is only temporary. We may have to find and light another candle later. But for now, the problem is temporarily solved, even if this is at a tiny level. But it is working for us.

Why is it better to do this than to curse the darkness? First, because cursing the darkness does not end it. We will still be in the dark after we have finished cursing it. Second, the candle can really help us against the darkness. We will definitely feel better and be able to see… even if it is only in the immediate area around us.

That's great, but let's not be too easy about this. What exactly is "the candle" when horrible people are doing horrible things to us and the people we value, and we cannot find any way to stop them? At that moment our subconscious may be fired up and pushing us to hate and attack our enemies. But that will not make us feel better.

Quite the reverse! If we instead stop and look for "the candle" then we will have redirected our minds towards finding a solution, no matter how small. This will already be making us feel better than our subconscious was doing a moment ago.

But, "the candle" has to actually work against the darkness. If we cannot find one that works then we will return to being upset. What candles can we use?

CANDLES FOR DARK TIMES 🕯

1. When We Are Losing Our Lives 🕯

This is the worst-case scenario. We, and the people we value, are losing our lives. If there is no quick and easy way to stop the horrible people then we may need a candle to help us get through the next few moments. Since the horrible people are killing us then our candle must help us to feel alive!

One way to do this is to sing together. People taking refuge in bomb shelters have cheered themselves up by singing their national anthem or a well-known song together. If you can do something like this then it is a candle that can help you to feel better for a while.

Another way is to go to a show. Even during a war, people have found relief by attending shows. These can help take their minds off their troubles for a while.

A third way is to put up a sign like "Business as usual", and then carry on with our work. Keeping work going is a candle that makes us feel better in spite of "the darkness" that surrounds us.

What if your loved ones have just been killed? What if your home has just been blown up and you are the only survivor? What candle can you use then? This time the candle must help you to feel that your loved ones are "still alive" in some way.

For some of us this will mean that their spirit is carrying on. We will have to remind ourselves about this and say our farewells, as their time spent with us on earth has ended. For other people there is no spirit. They will have to make a memorial of some kind for those who have been lost. "Keeping the loved ones in our thoughts and memories" is a candle that could help them here.

If it is your own life that is in danger then the candle that you need is for your own life to continue in some manner. One way is to remember your God, or spirit ancestors, or whatever works for you. This might be a good time to pray to them for the deliverance of your soul. If you don't have any supernatural beliefs then you could think of the other people who will remember you when you are gone. They will keep your memory alive.

After you have lit these candles then you may have time to think of something more effective that you could do about the murderous horrible people. I hope there is something you can find.

2. When We Are Losing Our Livelihoods

Another awful thing that horrible people can do to us and the people we value is to ruin our livelihoods. We have worked hard and built up our wealth but the horrible people have decided to wreck that. They may have stolen from us, tricked us, fired us, raised the interest rates, or put up the prices. Whatever method they have used, we are now worse off. If we can't think of a quick and easy way to fix this situation then we may need to "light a candle", at least for a while. We need a candle that helps us to feel well off!

One way to feel well off is to cut our spending. If we can live on less then we won't feel as much of the pain. This can keep us going until we get back on our feet.

Another candle we could use is to take some time off. If we can take some leave then we can forget about the horrible bosses and their horrible organization for a while. Let's worry about all that later. A break will do us good.

If we are forced to downsize then we can take this as an opportunity to make some beneficial changes in our lives. Maybe we will enjoy moving to a new area. Maybe we can sort out all the junk that we have been keeping for all these years! This could be a good time to rethink our priorities. We may be able to gain from this.

These are examples of the kind of "candles" that we can light to help us feel better for a while. Then we can focus on what we can do to improve things again.

3. When We Are Losing Our Freedoms
⊘

Sometimes it seems that horrible people could not live with themselves unless they were taking away someone else's freedoms. It's as if they get up in the morning and think: "What can we do to harm other people today?"

What candle can we light when our freedoms are being taken away from us and the people we value and we cannot find any way to prevent it? We need a candle that helps us to feel free, if only for a while.

One way is to do something that we want to do, but it is not banned yet. We can enjoy the freedoms we still have… while they last.

Another way is to do something that we are not allowed to do, but in secret. If we can find a safe way to do the banned thing then we can feel better about that for a while.

A third candle is to escape within our own minds. The horrible people don't have any "thought police" yet, so they can't control what we are thinking. We can enjoy these little breaks from the oppressive world we are living in, for a while.

These little candles can help us to feel better. After that we can search for ways to permanently escape from these oppressive horrible people with their horrible organizations and countries.

4. More Candles ☼

Horrible people can and do come after us in multiple ways in order to ruin our lives. That is what they live for. Well, at least it seems that way! Here are some other candles that you can use to feel better about them.

🕯 Do something you enjoy, even if it is a simple thing like getting a cup of tea or coffee. It's one good thing to add to your day.

🕯 Take a short break. A moment away from the horrible people will do you good.

🕯 Daydream… if you can get away with it!

🕯 Briefly remember one of the happier times in your life. Not everything is bad all the time.

🕯 Plan a future vacation. It's something to look forward to.

🕯 Work on your hobby. A pleasurable activity takes your mind off things.

🕯 Join a group. Time spent with people you share an interest with counterbalances the time you have to spend with horrible people.

🕯 Read a good book, see a movie, go to a show, do a crossword puzzle, attend a game... add these little happy moments to your life.

🕯 Chat with your friends.

🕯 Meditate, do some exercise, play a sport.

All these little candles can help us to feel better for a while, even though "the darkness" still surrounds us.

THE "NOT SO HORRIBLE" OTHER PEOPLE 👥

Not everyone is a horrible person. In fact, most people are quite okay. But that doesn't mean that they always make us feel better! Even the people we like can do things that annoy us, or that we don't agree with. What can we do to feel better then?

1. Put Things into Perspective 🔭

The not-so-horrible person is annoying us. We accept that. But do we have to feel so strongly about it? After all, we have agreed that this is *not* a horrible person. In that case their annoying behavior will not really hurt us. It is not a serious matter. Why not learn to ignore it, or at least to not take it so seriously? Why be concerned about so small a thing?

By putting their not-so-horrible behavior into perspective we can make ourselves feel better.

2. Look the Other Way 🌙

Another way to feel better about annoying or disturbing behavior is to look the other way or ignore it. If we are not paying attention to it then it can't stir up our feelings as much.

3. Remind Yourself of Their Good Points 🙋

They are not a horrible person so they definitely have their good points. Remind yourself of this. If you know the person well then you will be able to remember some of the good things they have done. Recall these good things and anything else that you like about this person. Their unlikable behaviors will soon become less upsetting and you will feel better.

4. Keep an Open Mind 📖

I know that you already do this. But it is still true that when a person has a very different background and behaviors to our own we can feel uncomfortable. We can make ourselves aware that this can happen and then remind ourselves to keep an open mind about other people's differences. They may dress very differently, have different customs, speak a different language, and so on, but they are really the same as us. They are not horrible people, they are just us from a different environment. These thoughts will make us feel better.

5. Understand Them 🕯

If someone's behavior is disturbing you then you may be able to help yourself to feel better by learning why they act like that. This is a risky approach because you will have to spend some time thinking about the disturbing behavior, which could make you feel worse for a while! But if you are up for it then learning why someone does something *may* help you to feel better about this type of behavior in the future.

6. Ask Them to Change

This is one of the riskiest things you could do to try to feel better. Asking someone to change does not create good feelings while you are doing it. And their response may make matters even worse! I recommend doing this only when you know the other person really well and are certain that they would willingly accept this request from you.

You may wonder why it is so hard to ask other people to change without it causing bad feelings. I will explain. Earlier I said that people like people who like and respect them. When you ask someone else to change it can make them feel that you don't like and respect them. They may then decide that they don't like and respect you in return.

Asking them to change will only have antagonized them and turned them against you. You will not be creating better feelings now!

How, then, can you get someone to change without it causing bad feelings? You have to get across that you like and respect the other person before you seek any change from them. This is why we have manners. Good manners tell the other person that you respect them and are politely asking them to do something, or to forgive you for what you just did, or are about to do, and so on. Good manners are the oil that makes the wheels of human interaction run smoothly. But how can you ask someone to change their behavior without it turning into "bad manners"… and without it making you feel worse too?

The well-known techniques are to act friendly, show respect, put the blame on yourself for making the request, talk about how you corrected your own (similar) faults – without ever mentioning theirs, tell a funny story about some remote person who had the fault, and so on. However, I am not sure that any of these will make you feel better.

The last way to get people to change is to have some authority over them. Most people will accept instructions from someone with authority, (but only if they are the type of instructions that the person is authorized to give). People will also accept instructions from people they like and respect. They give those people "the authority" to give the instructions *because* they like and respect them. If you are in such a position then you may be able to ask some people to change without it causing bad feelings all around!

Generally, I recommend avoiding telling other people to change, if you want to feel better. That is, unless you know them really well and are absolutely certain it will be okay with them!

The approaches we have discussed can help us to feel better in spite of the huge challenges that we face with some people. But why do we find these challenges so difficult in the first place? Let's look at that in the next chapter.

6. LOOKING FOR THE BAD

"Looking for the bad will never make you feel better!"

Why do we spend so much of our time looking for what's bad? Because it is a natural thing to do. As we discussed earlier, our minds were designed by nature to look for problems and then to try to solve them. It had to be this way, because nature wanted us to survive. Our subconscious is a major player in this, as it is the most animal-like part of our minds. As I said before, it is like an ancient animal which has developed over billions of years. Its idea to "Help me and my kind to survive!" is what starts us off on our search for everything that is bad about our world.

Imagine that we were designed by nature to only look for everything that is good. We would feel a lot better then. But we would not live for long! The bad things would soon get us. It was realistic of nature to not design us that way. Nature was a lot more practical than this and so designed us to pay special attention to the bad. That way we lived longer… but it also meant that we naturally felt worse about our lives.

How does this search for the bad work in our minds?

1. Our Emotions 😢

Our emotions are designed to be especially triggered by bad events. Bad events force us to experience strong negative emotions, such as fear, anger, hatred and disgust. These emotions then set our minds racing to find fast, effective solutions. We *desperately* want to get out of this bad situation that we have found ourselves in. Nothing else is more important to us at this time. Everything else is put on hold until we can find our way out.

Later, our emotions come back to us again and again, as they force us to reexamine what happened. We *have to* find a more effective solution. We *must* go over and over this bad event until we completely solve it and *will never* have to suffer from it again. That is what our emotions want the rest of our mind to do.

This does not feel good. And it takes no account of the fact that the bad event may never be able to be fully solved. The world can be like that – but the emotions don't care. They want an infallible solution now!

We feel bad.

2. Our Subconscious

Our subconscious joins in with the emotions. It starts to think about all the details of what happened and what went wrong. It pulls up memories of everything related to this event. Everything in our lives that might be related is brought to our attention. Surely with all this attention and information we should be able to solve the problem! At least, that is the view of the subconscious.

The subconscious feeds its concerns up to the conscious mind. It wants the conscious mind to get involved and come up with an answer. After all, that is what it is there for, isn't it? It's supposed to be the smart leader of the brain. If it is so smart then why isn't it providing an effective solution now!

3. Our Conscious Mind 💡

The conscious part of the mind receives these messages from the emotions and the subconscious and feels that it must react. This is a serious and difficult matter which must be solved. And right now! As soon as possible. Even if the event is over and the emotions and subconscious are just bringing it up again, the conscious mind feels the urgency of the demands and believes that everything else must wait until this is solved. A complete and perfect answer must be provided now, right away! Nothing else matters.

The conscious mind feels bad... especially when it cannot provide this magical, perfect answer right now.

And how could it? There is no magical, perfect answer to all the problems of the world. If there was we wouldn't have any problems in the world today. Obviously.

When the conscious mind tells the subconscious that it does not have a perfect answer to the problem right now then the subconscious is disappointed and gets mad. If the conscious mind refuses to solve the problem then the subconscious knows what to do! Kill, destroy, fight, devastate. These are the sort of answers that the subconscious comes up with. Then it goes back to the conscious mind saying that it had better carry out the "kill" command or else!

The conscious mind may be hypnotized by the forcefulness of this command and look for real ways to "kill" the problem person or situation. Real ways that could actually be carried out, without it turning into a major problem for us to survive! This may be to curse the problem, that is, to "curse the darkness", if you will. And we know how pointless that is. But what can we do instead? "Light a candle", maybe, but will that work here, with all the commotion that is going on inside our minds?

The subconscious is on the rampage now and it looks like there is no way to stop it. But there is a way. It is to answer its needs, as we have discussed before. We have to tell it that there is no effective solution to this problem right now, we have to find a way to live with what has happened, not everything in life is bad, and we commit to looking for better solutions in the future.

Hopefully, this will help the conscious part of our mind to regain control of the whole of the mind for a while. We can then consider how important this problem is in our lives right now. If it is genuinely very important then we should make time to find better answers for it. But if it is not as important or urgent as our feelings and subconscious have been saying then we can put it aside to be looked at later, at a more suitable time.

WHEN DO WE LOOK FOR THE BAD? 🔬

The search for what is bad in our lives and the world starts whenever we are experiencing something bad. That makes us pay a lot of attention. We are designed to pay close attention to anything that is bad because those things could go against our survival. Afterward, our minds are designed to return to thinking about the bad whenever we have a moment to ourselves. When we are not busy, or are doing something routine which doesn't require our full attention, our minds are naturally designed to start thinking about everything that has gone wrong in our lives, and also to worry about what might go wrong in the future. Our idle moments and our routine moments turn into nightmares of bad feelings as we remember the worst and worry about experiencing more of the worst!

What can we do to fix this? Some experts say that we should focus on the present. If we are always focusing on the present then worries about the past and the future cannot bother us. These experts advise us to meditate and "be mindful" of the present so that we can feel better all the time. But when will we learn from the past? And when will we make sensible plans for the future? Realistically, we need to do both of those things. How can we be realistic without also feeling worse?

The simple solution is to learn from the past and then forget about what happened. Remember the lessons and stop returning to the events. You can spend your quieter moments remembering what you want to remember, rather than what your subconscious wants to obsess about. For the future, you can make plans about what to do and leave it at that. Maybe some things will go wrong in the future. In fact, you can bet on that happening, as we have discussed before! But once you have planned everything that you can reasonably do about the future then you should "forget about" what may go wrong. Instead, think about the things you *want* to think about, and feel better.

WHAT KIND OF BAD FEELINGS CAN WE HAVE?

Bad feelings are not only about anger. We can also experience fear, hatred and disgust. This can be about other people or it can be about ourselves. It can also be about other things in the world. Whenever we see any of these bad feelings arising in our minds we can put ourselves on alert that they may try to take over our thoughts.

1. Fear

Fear drives a lot of our actions, even if we don't want to admit it to ourselves. It feels better if you don't realize that you are afraid yet still take action to avoid the danger! If you find that your thoughts are returning again and again to what can go wrong with something then fear will be driving them. Be alert to this so that you can take action to feel better instead.

2. Hatred 😒

Hatred is related to anger. It tells us that we want to kill or destroy the hated person or thing. It can drive us to "go to war". But this is rarely the best solution. Often it is better just to get away and then stay away from the hated person or thing! When you feel hatred then be on the alert for it trying to take over your mind and make you continue to feel bad.

3. Disgust 😧

Disgust is like hatred but in this case you do not want to touch the object of your disgust. You wouldn't mind if the disgusting person or object was destroyed, but you want to keep your distance from them or it at the same time. Destroy but do not touch! Be on the alert when you feel this way as the disgust may be trying to take over your mind.

4. Anger 😬

Good old-fashioned anger is the sovereign of all negative emotions. It is their ruler. It *demands* that something be done about the troublesome item, and done *right now*. Be on the alert when anger comes into your mind because it definitely wants to take over and rule you!

5. Towards Yourself 😳

The fear, hatred, disgust or anger can be directed towards yourself. You can fear that your weaknesses will allow you to be overcome. You can hate who you are or what you have done. You can be disgusted by aspects of your own character. You can be angry with yourself for your failures. And so on. Be alert to any of these negative emotions being directed towards yourself. You can then take steps to prevent them from taking over your mind. You will be able to guide yourself so that you feel better.

6. Other Forms ☹

Negative emotions come in various forms. Other forms of fear include worry and concern. Other forms of hatred include contempt and dislike. Other forms of disgust include loathing and feeling nauseated. Other forms of anger include rage and irritation.

When directed at yourself these include low self-esteem, self-doubt, self-contempt and self-loathing.

Be alert to any of these forms of negative emotions as they may try to take over your thoughts. Once you spot them you will be able to take steps so that you can feel better!

"MY KIND" 👶

The subconscious wants "me and my kind to survive". But who is it thinking of and what does it find when it looks for the bad that can happen to "my kind"?

As we discussed before, for the subconscious "my kind" is anyone who is similar to itself and is in "its group". When the subconscious is looking for what can go wrong in the world it includes what can go wrong for its kind. Anyone or anything outside that group can be ignored. As a result, the subconscious has strong feelings only for the benefit of whomever or whatever it thinks are its own kind. This is obviously dangerous.

Our conscious mind can be a lot smarter about this than our subconscious. It can see that other kinds of people may really be members of "our group". But this does not make the subconscious focus on these other people. Its interest is always focused on itself and its kind. It will only generate strong emotions about the problems that affect "its people". It will only force itself onto the conscious mind to demand answers to all of *its people's* problems. Everyone else will be ignored.

Your conscious mind can expect to receive anger, fear, hatred and disgust related to what is bad for "us". The anger can be directed at those who are "not us", especially if it looks like they might cause problems for our group. It can also receive fear about these "outsiders", with their strange ideas and ways. It can receive disgust related to their alien customs and appearances. Finally, it can receive hatred directed at these "foreign types", and the like. All this should be rejected by our conscious minds. But we should also be aware that it will happen within our minds, no matter what our more reasonable side thinks.

This is another area where we can be alert to our negative emotions. Dislike of foreigners and other "outsiders" will not make us feel any better. Our conscious mind can take steps to redirect these ideas towards wiser and more realistic ones. Then we will be able to feel better about the broader world we live in!

7. FIXING AND IMPROVING THINGS

"Fix what you can, when this will make you feel better."

Fixing and improving things are obvious ways to feel better. The trouble is we can't fix and improve everything in our lives or in the world today. Also, sometimes the fixing or the improving is way too hard, or not worth the effort to us. We are forced to choose which ones are worth getting involved in. Still, if fixing or improving something *is* worth the effort then that is a great way to feel better!

What worthwhile things could we successfully fix or improve in our lives?

NOT RECOMMENDED 🚳

As we discussed in the first chapter, the following are not worth the effort, will not work, and will not make us feel better in the long run.

1. Trying to Arrange a Perfect Life ✨
2. Getting Things 📱 + 🖥 + 🚗 (Or 👗 + 👠 + 👜)
3. Putting Your Happiness in the Hands of a Special Person 💖
4. Relying on Your Friends 😎😁😆
5. Pursuing Power 👑
6. Fooling Yourself 🤪
7. Trying to Be Perfect 😇
8. Keeping Busy 😕
9. Following Your Dreams ✳
10. Compromising 🙁

But these could be made more reasonable. Then they would work, be worth the effort, and make us feel better over the long run.

IMPROVED VERSIONS 🚶

1. Make Simple Improvements to Your Life 🔨
2. Get Simple Things ☕ 🛌 🍴
3. Be Reasonable with Your Partner 💋
4. Spend Time with Your Friends ☺☺☺
5. Be a Reasonable Person with Others ☺
6. Be Kind to Yourself ☺
7. Be Understanding Towards Yourself ☺
8. Do Worthwhile Things 👍
9. Pursue Your Interests 👣
10. Be Reasonable about Life ☼

Let's look at these in more detail.

1. Make Simple Improvements to Your Life 🔨

Simple improvements to your life will make you feel better. They will be easy to achieve. They are also very likely to work out well for you. Why wouldn't you do them!

Examples of simple improvements are endless. They include things like redecorating a room, taking a modest vacation, learning about something that interests you, gaining a new skill or working on one you have, trying out a new sport or game, and so on. You get the idea. All these simple improvements are well worth adding to your life. Choose the ones that interest you and go for it!

2. Get Simple Things

Pursuing the next big thing puts you on an endless, expensive and difficult treadmill where the better feelings never last. But pursuing the simple things is easy and affordable. Even if the better feelings need another boost after some time, they are super easy to achieve!

3. Be Reasonable with Your Partner

You may not be able to attain a "perfect synchronized love" with your partner, but you will be able to make yourself more reasonable with them. Both of you are real human beings, so you are sure to have your differences. Some aspects of yourself and your partner are never going to match. You cannot fix this... and why should you? Better to allow your partner to be themselves and for you to practice the simpler art of allowing for and tolerating their differences. They don't have to be perfectly matched to you, and you don't have to be perfectly matched to them. Instead, you can both be respectful and tolerant towards each other. This is the simpler thing that *can* be achieved. It will make both of you feel better.

Another simple thing that you can do is to be fair with your partner. Share the workload in the home. Help with the children (or the pets, or the plants!). Try to balance life's demands on each other. Appreciate what each of you do to support your family and your home. Both of you will feel better about your relationship!

4. Spend Time with Your Friends ☺☺☺

"You can't meet all of your friends all of the time, and you can't meet all of your friends some of the time, but you can meet some of your friends some of the time." And that last one is a simple thing to do. Spend some time with your friends when you can and this will bring some better feelings into your life!

5. Be a Reasonable Person with Others ☺

Rather than trying to gain power over others, you can pursue the simpler improvement of trying to be reasonable with other people. It is easier to be reasonable because this can be done at any level of society. You do not need to struggle to gain power. Even if you have some power, you should lighten up on being nasty to other people and bossing them around, at least because this won't make you feel better in the long run! If you want to feel better then knowing that you are being reasonable with other people will make that happen. If you don't have power, being reasonable with others will still work to make you feel better. It's a simple, effective solution.

What if the other people are not reasonable to you in return? Then you probably want to move on from them. It sounds like you are dealing with those "horrible" types who are best avoided, wherever possible!

Normal people *like* people who try to treat them reasonably.

6. Be Kind to Yourself ☺

You don't need to fool yourself in order to feel better. Instead, you can use the more reasonable approach of learning how your mind works and what you can do to help it feel better. You can understand that your subconscious has its ancient needs, and then look for ways to answer those in a reasonable way, as we have discussed before. Rather than trying to fight yourself or fool yourself, you can use the more effective approach of understanding and guiding yourself. You can be your own best leader – one that understands and truly wants what's best for you!

7. Be Understanding Towards Yourself ☺

Similar to being kind to yourself, you can be understanding about your limitations and the difficulties you face in this world. Life is not easy, and knowing the best thing to do all the time is not always obvious. You can forgive yourself for the things you got wrong or did not know at the time. You don't have to be perfect. You just need to learn from your experiences and move on. The simple approach of seeing yourself as a normal human being who is doing the best that they can will make you feel better.

8. Do Worthwhile Things 👍

You don't have to make yourself busy all the time in order to forget about feeling bad. You can simply add some worthwhile activities into your life. What makes something "worthwhile"? Whatever is worthwhile to you. It's not what other people say is worthwhile, it's what you say. (Even if that does agree with what other people say!) When you have added some simple worthwhile activities into your life then even when you are relaxing or having some idle time you will not feel bad about it. You will know that you have done something worthwhile and that is enough. You will feel better about your life.

9. Pursue Your Interests 👣

You may not be able to achieve all of your dreams, but you can spend some time pursuing what interests you. This will make you feel better, because you will have done something that you value. Life forces many activities onto us, which can leave us feeling drained and out of control. You can balance these by adding activities that you are interested in. Even if these activities do not take you to the top, they will have been worthwhile. You will have done something that you wanted to do. Part of your life will have been reclaimed, and you will be able to feel better because of that.

10. Be Reasonable about Life ☼

Life may not be a bed of roses, but it is not all bad either. You may not achieve all of your goals, and plenty of unfortunate events will happen to you over the years, but there are plenty of good things in life as well. Remember those and try to be reasonable about the whole journey of life.

Compromising is not a good answer, but neither is catastrophizing. Seeing things as they really are by taking "a balanced view", if you will, is far better than either compromising or always looking at the worst. A reasonable person reminds themselves that there are good things in life as well, and so feels better about it all.

OTHER AREAS WE COULD FIX OR IMPROVE

Apart from what we have discussed already, there are many areas that we could consider fixing or improving in our lives so that we feel better. Some of these are:

1. Improve Our Appearance

If it would make us feel better then we could consider ways to improve our appearance. We don't have to be the best-looking person in the world, but little improvements can help us to feel better about ourselves. That is not to say that we *have to* do this sort of thing. If we are not interested in changing our appearance then that is our affair. But if we are interested then there is nothing wrong with making small improvements.

We can update our clothes, change our hairstyle, modernize our makeup, improve our posture… whatever interests us. Men could grow or remove their beards, mustaches, sideburns, and so on! Women could grow or cut their hair, and straighten, wave or curl it. (Men could do this too!) Hair can also be colored, streaked, highlighted, styled, permed… all sorts of changes.

Our body shape can be changed via healthy eating, moderate exercise, weight training, Pilates, yoga, and so on.

We can work on our wardrobe, find out what colors and styles suit us, check what we like that is in fashion, accessorize, ask a consultant, ask a tailor… the list is long.

The key to all of this is to do what is simple and enjoyable, and makes us feel better. If it is making us feel worse then it is not for us!

2. Improve Our Abilities 🏃

We have discussed this before. If it would make us feel better then we can select some of our existing abilities and work on improving them. We could do this via training, practice and/or education – whichever works best for us. As long as the journey of improving is enjoyable and straightforward for us, and makes us feel better, then, no matter what the final outcome, it is worthwhile to do.

3. Fix the Negative Impact of Other People on Our Lives 🙊

Other people can have a negative impact on our lives, as you know! Fixing this is an area that could make us feel better.

First we must try to remember that "It is smarter to calm down and find sensible solutions to the existence of people we don't like so that we can safely feel better each day of our lives." It's not always easy to remember this, especially when the people are causing us harm at the time. But a calmer mind is more likely to find the easier, more effective ways to feel better. I struggle with this as you do! But it is still the best approach to take… if we want to feel better.

We do not need to fix the situation when the other person could not cause any real damage to us or our loved ones… or even to "our kind". This problem can be "fixed" by us learning to ignore the annoying person.

Ignoring is best done by never seeing or looking at them again. But if that is not possible then minimizing contact is a sensible approach. And when you do have to be in contact with them, imagining that there is a wall between you and them in your own mind can help!

If the damage the other person could cause would be minor then we only need to take small steps to fix this. The minimum that could work to protect us and our loved ones is what we should aim for. Our subconscious may be calling out for more dramatic steps to be taken, such as attacking and destroying the opponent, but as these are not really necessary we will feel better if we simply avoid the problem.

If the minor damage has already occurred then our aim should be to fix the damage, if it is important enough, and move on. We can take steps to avoid the problem happening again in the future and not worry about it anymore. But if we cannot find a way to avoid the problem happening again then it is no longer a minor level problem.

If the problem is no longer minor, or it could cause real damage to us and our loved ones, then we obviously need more serious "fixes". To feel better we should still be aiming for the minimum solution that would protect us and our loved ones… (and possibly also "our kind", or people in general). Minimum fixes include things like taking out insurance, implementing security measures, carrying personal alarms, contacting the police, taking the person to court, and so on. These are all obvious, well-known solutions that could help us in most cases. When we have implemented such "fixes" we will feel safer and better about our position in life.

The worst cases are when the damage has already occurred and when we cannot find any simple way to avoid the problem happening in the future. It is difficult to feel better then! To feel better when the damage has already occurred we need to fix what we can, if necessary "light a candle", and generally move on with our lives. The other ideas in this book should help to rebalance our lives so that we feel better than we otherwise would have. But if we cannot find a simple way to avoid the problem happening in the future then we only have two main options. The first is to look for a more difficult solution, as there is no simple one available. We can then check if the more difficult solution is worth doing for us. If it is worth doing then we can proceed, even though we understand that it won't be easy. We will still feel better because "at least we are doing something worthwhile to us". If it is not worth doing then we can move on to the second main option. The second main option is to accept that the problem is unavoidable, as we have discussed before. There is no feasible or worthwhile way to fix it. We have to accept it and move on. Having accepted this, we can then add other things into our lives that will make us feel better in general. We can also balance the problem by remembering the good side, as we have talked about before.

Fixing the negative impact of other people on our lives is sometimes simple, sometimes more complex, and sometimes impossible. We can feel better by applying the simple fixes, applying the more complex ones when they are worthwhile to us, and by not trying to fix the impossible!

4. Improve Our Likability

We will never be able to get everyone to like us, but we can take simple steps to improve our likability. That way we will have fewer problems with most other people, which will make us feel better.

The basis of being more likable is to treat other people as if we like and respect them. We can learn the manners, looks and customs that tell other people that we like and respect them. Obviously these will be different for different people in different areas, but if we learn and apply the ones that are preferred by most of the people we are encountering then we will have gone a long way towards being more likable. There will always be someone who doesn't like the manners, looks and customs that are common to their area. All we can do for those people is to treat them as if we like and respect them too. It will never be perfect, but it is the best that we can do!

5. Prepare for Bad Events

Bad events will occur in the world and in our own lives. We can "fix" them by trying to prepare for them. If we have been able to prepare for bad events then we will feel better about our futures.

Although our subconscious naturally tends to look for the bad, it can be quite casual about preparing for the future. This is because it has a tendency to focus on what is happening today. But today might be the best time to prepare for our future. If we don't prepare then we may feel worse when the future problems come to meet us!

Simple things we can do to prepare for possible future bad events are to set some money aside in a nest egg, take out insurance, buy a home in a safe area (including safe from crime, flood, fire, earthquake, tsunami, hurricane, mudslides, and so on), keep an eye on the local political situation for signs of coming danger, ensure our skills are current for today's employment needs, contribute to a retirement fund, and so on. Simple preparations like these can help to reduce the impact of future bad events in our lives, making us feel better now and when any bad events do occur.

6. Reduce Our Risk of Getting Sick

We will get sick, but we can reduce the chances of it happening to us. We can also increase our ability to recover from some illnesses.

We discussed these "fixes" before: eat well, keep reasonably fit, get enough sleep, reduce stress, have regular medical check-ups, don't smoke, see the doctor early when we have serious or suspicious symptoms, and so on. These small but obvious steps will help us to keep as well as we can and will also make us feel better.

7. Reduce the Risk and Impact of Accidents ⚙

As we discussed before, we can reduce the risk and impact of accidents in our lives. Insurance could reduce the impact of an accident if it does occur. A nest egg could help us to recover from the accident. We can also reduce our accident risk by doing things like learning defensive driving, installing safety devices in our homes and workplaces, getting a good night's sleep, and so on. Such steps will make us feel safer about our future.

8. Reduce the Impact of Aging

We can reduce the impact of aging by eating well, keeping physically active, getting enough sleep, reducing stress, having regular medical checkups, not smoking, seeing the doctor early when we have serious or suspicious symptoms, and so on. These are the same things we did to reduce our chances and the impact of getting sick. We can add to those: keeping mentally active and keeping socially active. These activities can also help to reduce the impact of aging on our lives.

9. Reduce the Risk of Making Mistakes

We will make mistakes in our lives, but we can reduce the risk of doing this. The first way to reduce the risk of making mistakes is to learn from the ones that we already have made. Experience can be a great teacher. If we make it our habit to learn from what we got wrong then problems will be turned into gains.

The second way we can reduce the risk of making mistakes is to learn from other people's. We can listen to and learn from other people about what they got wrong and make sure that we don't fall into the same trap. We can also learn what other people did to get things right and apply that. Learning from both negatives and positives will reduce our own risk of making mistakes in the future. We can feel better because we have done that!

Fixing and improving what we can, when it is worthwhile to us, are great ways to feel better. But what can we do about the larger problems in the world that seem to be beyond our own power to fix? We will discuss that in the next chapter.

8. "UNFIXABLE" WORLD PROBLEMS

"What cannot be fixed must be ignored."

The world is filled with problems that we cannot fix on our own. Even the powerful leaders of the world seem to have trouble fixing them. How can we feel better when so much is going wrong and seems to be out of anyone's control? The only realistic thing we can do is to admit that this is the case. By admitting that the problems exist and cannot be overcome we will strangely feel better about them. We should then move on to the things that we *can* fix or improve, and also remind ourselves about the good side to balance our view.

But what about our subconscious mind? It wants us to solve all the problems of the world, especially the ones that it thinks could harm it and "its kind". If we tell it that there are unfixable problems then it will start to worry. The solution we discussed before when we could not find a workable way to answer the needs of our subconscious was to redirect its attention and commit to finding better answers in the future. But how can we find better answers to the world's problems when even the powerful world leaders can't do anything? When the subconscious realizes that we are not going to be able to lead it to a better and safer world for it and its kind then it will lose faith in us. It will look for ways to take control of the mind so that it can run the show. The results could be harmful to us and our lives, and we will not feel better. What can we do?

HELPING THE SUBCONSCIOUS TO ENDURE "UNFIXABLE" WORLD PROBLEMS ☹

1. Cut Back on Our News Feed ⚡

The subconscious is drawn to looking for the bad. If we feed it bad news then it will lap that up and worry a lot. The daily stream of bad news made available to us by the media will certainly draw the attention of the subconscious and give it plenty to be upset about. Anything that it identifies as potentially affecting its survival and the survival of "its kind" will worry it and eventually drive it crazy. The conscious mind should be aware of this issue and take charge to limit the flow of bad news. We cannot expect the subconscious to understand what is happening here. It is up to our conscious minds to protect the subconscious from itself.

We cannot completely stop looking at the world's bad news as we do need to keep an eye on the local situation for signs of coming dangers. We may need to take steps to protect ourselves from these. But most of the news is not about this. Most news is about remote events that we would never have known existed if it wasn't for the media. These won't affect us directly. Yet our subconscious will worry about them as if they were "right in our backyard". We need to limit what we show it to the minimum that is necessary for our actual safety and security. Then it will worry less.

2. Put the Problems into Perspective ☞

The conscious mind can help the subconscious in its understanding of the world's problems by pointing out their actual impact on it and its loved ones. Most of the world's "unfixable" problems do not affect us or our loved ones directly. If the conscious mind takes a moment to point this out then the subconscious will worry about these less.

The problems may affect "its kind", however. Whoever the subconscious has identified as "its kind" will come under its umbrella of people to worry about. In this case the conscious mind can check how close the affected people really are to the subconscious's definition of "its kind". If they are more remote then that will help the subconscious to worry less. This may seem callous, but we are only talking here about how the subconscious works. It works at a more animal level and so can be calmed by seeing that "its people" are not really affected. We can still do what we can to help the remote people, after we have calmed our subconscious down.

3. Look into the Distant Future 🔭

Will the unfixable world problems of today still exist in the far distant future? This is a question worth asking ourselves. If we find that some of the current problems may be fixed one day then our subconscious will start to feel a little better about them. It's not a perfect solution, obviously, because it is far away and will not solve things for us in our own lives. But it is a good thing to know.

Some problems will still seem unfixable even in the distant future. If we think that this is the case then looking into the future won't make us feel any better about them. But for the others it is a useful way to feel better.

4. Take Some Action 🔧

Even if we can't fix the unfixable world problems, if we take some small action about them we will feel better. We will feel that we have done something, rather than just ignoring the problem. Our small contribution may not have solved the problem, but it is a step in the right direction. We can feel good about what we have done.

5. Do Something Useful 👫

If there is a useful action about a world problem that we can take, and it is worthwhile to us to do, then we can pursue that. Being involved in an action that will help fix some of the world's problems will reduce our concerns about all the things that are going wrong today. Even if the impact of our actions will not be realized until long into the future, having been involved in them will make us feel better.

WHY ARE THERE WORLD PROBLEMS? 🔬

Understanding why the world has problems may be a way to help us to feel somewhat better about them. Also, it may help if we could understand why the powerful world leaders can't seem to fix them either. No one expects world leaders to fix problems like the fact that we all die, some diseases are incurable, accidents continue to happen, and so on. What we do expect them to fix are problems like the conflicts between nations, crimes still being committed, the instability of world economies, resources not being allocated where we need them… issues along these lines. Let's look at some of these problems.

1. Why Are There Still Conflicts between Nations? ✕

There are a lot of reasons, but the basic one is that people don't see the other people as being of "my kind". As you know, the subconscious automatically decides who is "my kind" based on things like their similarities to itself. If it thinks someone is not of "my kind" then it does not include them in its goal to "Help me and my kind to survive!" Almost anything can be done to the "not my kind of people" without the subconscious really caring. This is the basis of all conflict between nations.

Shared history, shared customs, shared beliefs… all manner of apparently shared appearances and ways tell the subconscious who to include and who to exclude. When a group of subconsciouses get together, feeling that they are all included in "our kind", then they can unashamedly allow a wide range of harmful actions to be carried out on the excluded "not our kind of people". If a horrible leader takes charge of the group then all manner of atrocities can follow.

Why can't the powerful world leaders fix this problem? Firstly, because it comes from the subconsciouses of their own people. It would be difficult to lead their people against the beliefs of their own subconsciouses. Secondly, because the world leaders have their own subconsciouses, which also have a view of who is included in "my kind". The leaders may not be able to see outside this narrow view themselves. The world leaders are consequently not empowered to take any action, and may not even see that there is anything to fix. Conflicts between nations will then continue.

But why can't the smarter conscious side of our minds stand up and correct these errors? Well, it can. But this doesn't happen often. What usually happens is that the view of our subconscious decides who to include and who to exclude from our care and attention. With so many people thinking like this the world will continue to be an unfair and even cruel place. But it is natural!

How does this understanding make us feel any better? Because the alternative is to wonder why there are still so many problems in the world and nothing serious is being done to fix them. This alternative view will make you feel frustrated and angry with the world and its leaders. You will also worry more about the future. But now that you understand the natural subconscious cause of the ongoing problems, and the seeming inability of the powerful world leaders to fix them, you can feel *slightly* better. It is still a shame that this is what is happening. It would be better if people's conscious minds could take over the judgment of who to include in "my kind". But it is understandable that this is not the case.

Having understood the cause of the conflicts and unfairness between nations we can then seriously consider "throwing it in the trash", where it belongs. This is from step one of the plan we previously discussed for feeling better:

1. Admit that some bad things will always happen no matter what we do… and then move on from this point. 🗑

2. Fix or improve what we can, where we can… when it is worth the effort to us.

3. Look at the genuine good side… realistically balance the bad with the good.

2. Why Are Crimes Still Being Committed?

The basic reason is that the criminals see their victims as either not being of "their kind", or as the enemies of their kind. This allows them to carry out their criminal actions without worrying about their victims or feeling guilty. They may even feel that they are justified.

The powerful world leaders cannot stop all the crime in their own countries because there are always people who feel this way – that their victims are not their kind or are their enemies. The leaders would have to find a way to change the feelings of everyone in their society. Every person would have to believe that all the other members of their nation were "their kind". This is impossible for a leader to achieve.

Why don't criminals see all the other members of their nation as of their kind? For the same reason that none of us do. The reality is that we only see some of the people around us as truly being of our kind. The rest are like strangers. Our subconscious does not feel strongly attached to them. Some of the people around us can even be seen as enemies. We can all imagine committing crimes against them!

As long as people's subconsciouses continue to see some people as not being of "their kind", crime will continue in our world.

Having understood the inevitability of this situation we can happily toss it in the trash can!

3. Why Are Our World Economies Still Unstable? 🌿

This looks like a different kind of problem. Our powerful world leaders seem to be unable to stabilize the world's or even our own nation's economy. Why is this?

The basic cause is that some people compete with each other and are unfair. If all people treated each other fairly then there would be no problem with the world's economies. But that is impossible. People will always treat some people as not being of their kind, or as being less important members of their kind. The resulting competition and mistreatment leads to swings in prices, pay, quality of services provided, and so on. The swings move values back and forth, resulting in inflation, interest rate hikes, wage demands, retrenchments, foreclosures, outsourcing, bankruptcies, and so on. World leaders can work to dampen down the movements, but they cannot completely control them. The result is what we see today.

The situation could be worse. Economists have learned how to dampen the movements of the economy over the years. This has meant less issues for the world's economies. But they have been unable to solve everything, because this basically comes from the way people treat each other.

Having understood all this, we can throw it in the trash can with the rest of the rubbish!

4. Why Aren't Resources Allocated Where We Need Them? ✠

If some people are going to treat other people as not being of their kind, or as being less important members of their kind, then how could resources be allocated where everyone really needs them? It's impossible. Due to the nature of people's subconscious judgments about the relative importance of other people – unfairness, callousness, nastiness and selfishness will all follow. How could the world's leaders solve this... if they even wanted to? They would need to change *nearly everyone's* human nature. Impossible.

An alternative solution would be to take away the power from anyone who did not include all human beings as "their kind". But that is just about everyone. World leaders do not have the power or will to do that.

A different solution is to let leaders compete with each other. This is what we do in democracies today. The result is that the allocation of resources will move back and forth as each leader takes control and is then replaced. One leader will allocate resources to one group of "their kind", and the next one will reallocate the resources to a different group. That way the resources keep moving around, in spite of the subconscious limitations of the leaders and their supporters. It sounds crazy, I know, but that is basically what we do in our democratic systems. It is better, though, than letting only one leader decide where resources will be allocated, especially if they don't include us in the group of "their kind"!

As with the other "unfixable" world problems that we have been looking at, this resource allocation one is down to the nature of people's subconsciouses. Let's look at that in more detail.

WHY CAN'T PEOPLE'S SUBCONSCIOUS NATURE BE FIXED? 🔨

As we discussed before, the subconscious is that huge area of your mind that is "below the surface". You can't see it, but it is there. The world's problems, by which we mean the world's problems between people, mostly come from this huge unseen area of their minds. The most critical part of the problem is in how the subconscious decides where other people sit in relation to itself. Its goal is to "Help me and my kind to survive!" Naturally this results in itself and the people closest to it being the ones it wants to get the most support "to survive". After that it includes the next closest, and then the next, and lastly the more distant people. It assigns lesser and lesser levels of support as the distance (or difference to itself) increases. Finally, it sees any people who endanger its own and its chosen people's survival as enemies. Its natural view is that enemies should be avoided, defeated or destroyed.

Most people's subconscious views about who is included in "my kind" can be changed by their experiences. But most of the time their experiences are similar to what has happened to them before, so their subconscious view does not change.

Some subconsciouses have a very narrow view of who is in "their kind". They see a lot more people as being undeserving of their support. They also see a lot more people as enemies. These subconsciouses can be very dangerous to the rest of us. This is where the "horrible people" and the "horrible leaders" come from.

Why are some subconsciouses like this? For natural reasons. It can be their experiences or it can be that they were born like that, or it can be a combination of both. Why they are like this is not the important question. The important question is could they be changed? Yes, sometimes. Just as it is with the "not so horrible" people, later experiences can help horrible people to change their views. But the chances of this happening are small. They almost always remain horrible.

How can we feel better about any of that? By accepting it: that this is the case. There will always be problems between the people of the world, and this will especially apply where the "horrible people" are involved. Throw that in the trash can and move on!

9. HUMOR

"Laughter can hurt."

Can humor make you feel better? At first you might think yes. But sometimes after you have finished laughing you can feel worse. Why is that?

WHEN DOES HUMOR MAKE YOU FEEL WORSE? 😬

1. When It Upsets the Subconscious ☹

The subconscious enjoys humor too. It is not just the conscious mind which can laugh. The subconscious has a sense of humor, just as it has the ability to be creative.

The problem starts when the joke is about something negative. It makes us feel better about the negative thing for a moment, because now we can laugh at it. That's great. But after we have finished laughing, the subconscious soon realizes that the problem has not gone away. It has not been solved. Laughter has merely diverted us for a while. Since the problem remains, the subconscious must return to feeling bad about it.

Even hearing the joke can make us feel worse, because we were not thinking about the negative thing before. Now that we are paying close attention to it, in order to hear and enjoy the joke, we have brought it firmly into our minds. We have placed a negative thing right in the middle of our view. And we are staring at it. That is not a way to feel better!

It would be better to never hear the joke at all. Then our minds will not be focused on the negative and we can move on. Leave the negative in the trash, I recommend.

2. When It Doesn't Solve the Problem ☺

Humor can seem to solve a problem. Yet it does not actually do so. It gives us a comical answer to the things in life that upset us. We laugh at the surprise answer. If only it were true. But it is not true. It is ridiculous. After we finish laughing we will realize this and be left with the problem.

Humor can seem to provide support to us, as we can be surrounded by people who are sharing the laughter with us. Surely they are aware of the same problems that we face in our lives? That is why they are laughing with us. We are not alone. But doesn't this mean that all of us are failing to solve our problems? We share them, but so what? There are no solutions being offered here. Maybe it's harmless to at least laugh together at what we could not solve. But, on the other hand, we are now paying attention to this. What's the use of that? It won't make us feel any better after the laughter has ended. Better to move on.

3. When It Introduces Us to a New Problem 😱

We could be sailing along, happy in our lives, and then we hear a joke. The joke could be about a new problem that we have never heard of before. How will we feel?

At first we may be fascinated by the joke. This is a new style of humor, or a new subject for us. How interesting! We may laugh longer and louder than we ever did before, because this was such a surprise. Great! And then? And then we will be aware of a new negative thing in our lives: one we had never thought of before. We can now "enjoy" knowing about something else that is wrong with our world.

One "great" thing about humor is that it can be so memorable. The twist in a good punchline can stay with us for years. After we have heard it we are committed to returning to the joke time after time. It keeps popping back into our minds. And that means the new negative will also keep popping back into our minds. Wonderful! Thanks a lot for *that* joke. I think not.

WHAT'S GOOD ABOUT HUMOR? 😊

Surely there must be something good about humor. Otherwise, why do we keep doing it?

We have been designed to laugh. It is our nature to look for things that are funny, in the same way that we look for surprising new answers to problems. We enjoy answers which reveal a completely new way to look at a problem which makes it simple to solve. The issues we have been facing evaporate in an instant. What a fantastic new answer! If only we had thought of it before. But now we are free – liberated from this long-standing issue.

Nature designed us this way. It is one of the secrets of humanity's success. We find pleasure in new, surprising answers. That is what makes us laugh when we hear a good joke. There is nothing wrong with laughing like that. But… not when the joke ends up making us feel worse!

On the other hand, if the joke could somehow make us feel permanently better about the problem then that would be a good joke. We would want to keep hearing jokes like that.

WHAT HUMOR WOULD MAKE US FEEL PERMANENTLY BETTER? ☺

The humor that answered our problems. It's not the joke that matters, it is the solution it offers. If a joke offers a workable, realistic solution to our problems then it is a joke worth hearing. But where is the need for humor in that?

We don't need our workable, realistic solutions to be funny. We need them to work. If they happen to be completely new ways to look at our problems which make them simple to solve then they may feel funny to us. They may remind us of jokes. But they will also be *actual* solutions to our problems, not just amusing tricks that leave us still badly off.

This doesn't mean that we can't enjoy a good joke that doesn't really solve anything but doesn't make us feel worse. There is no harm in that. It is only when the joke reminds us of the insoluble problems we have, and continues to remind us long into the future, that it is a joke we could have done without!

WHEN SHOULD WE MAKE A JOKE, AND WHEN SHOULD WE JUST "TRASH IT"? 🗑

Joking about bad things, such as our enemies, our problems and our failings, may seem like a harmless way to lighten the mood. Why can't we do that and then later "trash the problem"? Wouldn't that be more fun than just accepting that the problem exists and then throwing it in the trash?

Not if you want to feel better. Laughing may feel good for a while, but it won't work for the long term. Better to laugh at things that won't make you feel worse, and forget about (or solve) the ones that would. If you do laugh at something that could be solved, and then solve it afterward, that could be okay too.

THE DANGER OF USING HUMOR INSTEAD OF SOLVING THINGS ↻

Humor makes us feel better for a while. This is because our minds have been designed to enjoy solving problems, especially when the solution is a surprise one. These better feelings can become a substitute for actually solving our problems in life.

If we choose to use humor instead of solving what can be solved then we can become trapped. Since the good feelings do not last, we will be forced to recreate them again and again. It will become one of those endless treadmills that we have to keep returning to in order to feel good. Just like relying on buying expensive things, trying to make our lives perfect, or chasing after power, we will have to return to our treadmill and make it turn, over and over again. It is a "solution" that cannot last.

If we instead choose to solve what can be solved, then we will be able to overcome those problems forever! Fixing and improving things can work in some areas of our lives. Fixing and improving things, where it is worthwhile to us, is a guaranteed way to feel better.

The rest, of course, can be trashed.

LIGHTENING UP ☺

I am not opposed to humor. I like it. I just wanted to help you to understand when it might be hurting you. Be aware of that and protect yourself. Otherwise, when it is not harmful to you, go ahead and enjoy a good joke!

10. DREAMS, INTERESTS AND WORTHWHILE ACTIVITIES

"Doing worthwhile things will make you happier."

Earlier in the book we said that there were better ways to feel happier than Keeping Busy and Following Your Dreams. These were to Do Worthwhile Things and Pursue Your Interests. How did this work?

1. Keeping Busy ☹

We know that keeping busy does not work because you have to stop sometimes and then your conscious mind will remember that you are not happy. Also, your subconscious will always be noticing that you are not happy and will drive you to feel bad even when you are busy.

2. Do Worthwhile Things 👍

Rather than making yourself busy all the time, you can add some simple worthwhile activities into your life. Knowing that you have done something worthwhile will make you feel better, even when you are relaxing or having some idle time. By "worthwhile" we mean whatever is worthwhile *to you*.

3. Following Your Dreams ✴

We know that following your dreams does not always work because you may not achieve your goals. Things can go wrong. Also, the steps on the way to your goal may be difficult and unenjoyable. If those steps don't really lead anywhere then what is the point in taking them?

4. Pursue Your Interests 👣

Rather than trying to follow your dreams, you can add some activities to your life that you are interested in. This will make you feel better because you will have done something that you value. You will have reclaimed part of your life.

But does all this make sense? What do these answers really mean? Are these areas really all that different from each other?

WHAT IS DIFFERENT BETWEEN DREAMS, INTERESTS AND WORTHWHILE ACTIVITIES? 🔍

Dreams, interests and worthwhile activities have a lot in common. All of them have some sort of goal. All of them take time and effort to do. All of them "advance you" in some way. What is different about them, especially in terms of making you feel better?

1. What Are Dreams? ✷

Dreams are something to aim for. Getting to them requires "a journey". They can require sacrifice and effort to get to. They can be very difficult to achieve. Realistically, for the "big" dreams there can be no guarantee that you will ever reach them.

If you achieve a dream you will feel great for a while, especially because of all the effort you have had to put in. But if you fail to achieve a dream then you could feel terrible because your efforts seem to have been wasted. You may also feel like "a failure".

2. What Are Interests? 👣

Interests are things that you want to be involved in. Rather than requiring a journey, *they are the journey*. They sometimes require sacrifice and effort, but you quickly feel good about this. They can be easy, okay or hard to do. Realistically, you will almost always enjoy them, no matter how hard they are.

Interests are "achieved" as soon as you are doing them. You cannot "fail" at an interest, even if it doesn't work out for you.

3. What Are Worthwhile Activities? 👍

Worthwhile activities are whatever you believe is worthwhile. They do not require a journey to get to, but they may put you on one! They ask for sacrifice and effort, but this will be acceptable to you. They can be easy, okay or hard to do. Realistically, you will want to do them if you really believe in them being appropriate for you.

Every worthwhile activity you are involved in will make you feel good. Whether your actions work out or not, you cannot "fail" at a worthwhile activity.

4. Which Ones Make You Feel Better... and When?

Dreams make you feel better when you achieve them... at least, for a while.

Interests make you feel better when you are doing them, even though they may frustrate you at times!

Worthwhile activities make you feel better for much of the time, but only if you really believe that they were worthwhile for you to do.

THEN WHICH ONES SHOULD YOU DO... AND WHEN?

1. Dreams

Dreams that cannot be achieved will only be worth doing if you still find "the journey" interesting or worthwhile. Otherwise they would be a waste of your time. They would only frustrate you. You would not feel better!

Dreams that could be achieved may be worth suffering for, if you find that your desire to achieve them outweighs the sacrifice, effort and difficulties that would occur on the journey. Remember: the good feelings that you will get when you achieve them will not last, no matter how intense they may be. Bear that in mind when deciding if the dreams are worth following.

Dreams that could be achieved and whose journey would be mostly enjoyable, interesting and worthwhile to you are obviously okay to pursue!

2. Interests 👣

Interests are worth doing if you find them interesting enough. If they will require any sacrifice or big effort then you can easily decide if you still want to pursue them by comparing this with how much interest you have in them.

The more an interest appeals to you the better it will make you feel.

3. Worthwhile Activities 👍

Worthwhile activities are worth doing based on how worthwhile they are to you. If you do not find them truly worthwhile for yourself to be involved in then, no matter what other people think, they are not for you! But if you do believe in doing them then you can compare that with how much sacrifice or effort they might require and decide if they are still worth it to you.

When you get involved in worthwhile activities that you believe are really worthy of your efforts then you will feel better for much of your day.

OTHER WAYS TO FEEL BETTER IN THE FUTURE 🚀

Apart from pursuing our dreams, interests and worthwhile activities, there are other actions that we could take to help us feel better in the future.

1. Ignore the Unfixable 🚶

There are some awful, inescapable truths that we can't fix or improve on. We could make it our habit to accept this and then turn away from them and ignore them. ☾

Also, if it would help us to feel better, we may choose to "light a candle 🕯", rather than "curse the darkness 👺".

2. Fix or Improve Things ⛏

When we have the power to do it, and we believe it will be worth the effort to us, we can fix and improve some areas of our lives.

Examples:

- Improve our skills and abilities. 🤸
- Teach ourselves to calm down and find sensible solutions to the existence of people we don't like so that we can safely feel better each day of our lives. 😌
- Remind ourselves that a person is not truly important just because they have worldly power, riches or great abilities. They are truly important when they bring benefits to the world. Also, if someone is unlikable then they are not an important person. Truly important people are always likable. 🌹

HOW TO FEEL BETTER... REALISTICALLY

- Learn what is considered good manners and an acceptable appearance among the people we are going to spend time with.

- Think about the ways we can show people that we like and respect them.

- Prepare for predictable disasters and bad events in our area.

- Look after our health.

- Take out insurance.

- Set aside some funds for emergencies.

- Learn defensive driving.

- Install safety and security devices in our homes and workplaces.

- Where possible, arrange to get a good night's sleep.

- Keep mentally and socially active.

- Learn from our mistakes and those of others. Also, learn from what other people got right.

- Look after the basic needs of our subconscious in a responsible, adult way. Also, occasionally search for better answers to its outstanding concerns.

- Learn to notice when we are having strong negative emotions so that we can stop, calm ourselves down, and look for sensible solutions to what is bothering our subconscious. 💣

- Consider who should really be included in the group of "our kind". We might like to study other cultures and different types of people to see if any of them could be added to our group. 👨‍🦰👩‍🦱👱‍♀️👮‍♂️👷‍♀️👨‍✈️👦👧👰

3. Remember the Good ⛄

Whenever we are noticing the bad things in life, make it our habit to also look at the genuine good side. Realistically balance the bad with the good. ⚖️

THE FINAL WORD

"You can feel better… realistically."

You now know multiple ways to feel better. All of them are based on being realistic. Being realistic is the best approach to feeling better because it is the only one that works over the long run. Every other approach fails at some point.

The person who is the most realistic is the most happy. They look for sensible answers that could really work. They don't try to fool their subconscious but instead face up to and accept the awful inescapable truths about life. This allows them to move on and feel better. When it is worthwhile to them, they fix and improve what they can. To balance the bad they remind themselves about the good side of life. In the worst cases they choose to "light a candle" rather than waste their time "cursing the darkness". They know how to feel better… realistically.

www.ingramcontent.com/pod-product-compliance
Lightning Source LLC
Chambersburg PA
CBHW070258010526
44107CB00056B/2495